HANA 1

花に関している詩

Stean Anthony

YAMAGUCHI SHOTEN

山口書店　京都

Character on the cover is an old Chinese character for flower a variant of the one below. There are other variants.

華

Mirror Reply

The word is love
The letter is love
The heart is love
The figure is love
The character is love.

Inspired by ancient mirrors
金粒珠玉象嵌宝相
華紋六稜鏡唐8世紀.

Hear my voice at:
<http://www35.tok2.com/home/stean2/>

HANA 1
©2018 Stean Anthony
Author's profits
See end of book for details
PRINTED IN JAPAN

FLOWERS
FOR FRIENDS
JAPAN KOREA
TAIWAN CHINA
RUSSIA PHILIPPINES
PACIFIC NATIONS
EUROPE AFRICA
WORLD

Seasons

Morning east evening west
The day goes round
On a circle in space
We live in a house
Tied to the sun.

HANA 1
Contents

Dedication poem Seasons: Morning east evening west		4
Preface		16
Preface Poem 華 Hana: If I count thy lines what shall I find		19
1.	Hanapoem 1: She asked me why	20
2.	Hanapoem 2: I'm drawing pictures to say	20
3.	Hanapoem 3: Born on a flower	20
4.	火花 Hibana: Tumbles from the quarry wall	21
5.	Anthesis: The fingers flicker through the light	21
6.	Karuta: Cut me up & spread me on the floor	21
7.	七草 Nanakusa 1: On the seventh day of January	22
8.	七草 Nanakusa 2: Seri 芹 green vigor	22
9.	七草 Nanakusa 3: The throne of charity	22
10.	七草 Nanakusa 4: Suzuna 菘 the white cloud	23
11.	櫻 Cherry: Mother gathered clams in the shallow water	23
12.	Asahi: I found an old poster	23
13.	黒松 Kuromatsu 1: The black pine on the white sand	24
14.	沖ノ島 Okinoshima 1: Holy dwelling of the guardian	24
15.	Almond: To greet the year in bridal white	24
16.	Family Flower: Observe the bud	25
17.	翡翠 Hisui: In the formation of the land	25
18.	玄米茶 Genmaicha: A tablespoon of light amber oil	25
19.	Bell Pepper: Looking at the bells	26
20.	Cockerel: White bantam with the scarlet wattle	26
21.	Mustard Chicken: In the hot olive oil	26
22.	絵島 Eshima: Cloudless night without wind	27
23.	Kuromame: Tangled bean vines heaped on rice poles	27
24.	Bourne by the Waves: Great islands sail upon the water	27
25.	牡丹鍋 Botan Nabe: Shall I be the beaters	28
26.	豆乳 Tōnyū: Still warm in the sealware beaker	28
27.	Tago no Ura: Walking along the shore	28
28.	Garlic Leaf: Harvest the green leaves at dawn	29
29.	Kimono Flower: Japonica printed on cream silk	29
30.	笠取山 Kasatori 1: From the heights of Kasatori	29
31.	笠取山 Kasatori 2: From the heights of Kasatori	30

32.	Era Name 1: The man held up the white sign	30
33.	節分 Setsubun: Start the seasons turning	30
34.	Yamata no Orochi 1: Our ancient dreams alive before us	31
35.	Yamata no Orochi 2: Eight wooden vats of perfumed wine	31
36.	Yamata no Orochi 3: Out of the sky realms bright-robed	31
37.	Era Name 2: The new name to follow tradition	32
38.	Era Name 3: That was the meaning of Heisei	32
39.	Spring Herbs: Mother Mãe gather herbs for family	32
40.	Flower Poetry: Take a deep breath	33
41.	Winter Jasmine 1: From my green sleeve my hand	33
42.	Kobe Waterfall: The heat fled to the sky	33
43.	Hasedera Festival 1: Brightly burn the fiery torch	34
44.	Coffee 1: Highland spring abundant flowers	34
45.	源信 Genshin: Great father with a flower soul	34
46.	Plum Blossom: Is there snow on the wall in the Kyoto garden	35
47.	Hasedera Festival 2: By the power of the word	35
48.	Heart Flower: Weather chart Japan is bright sun	35
49.	Kairakuen: Snow-white tabi on the goza	36
50.	Prunus: Absolutely gorgeous	36
51.	Winter Daphne: A heady musk	36
52.	お守り Omamori: He came to Brazil on the first boat	37
53.	Word Flower 1: To be as I ought	37
54.	Word Flower 2: Looking to an island	37
55.	鬼瓦 Onigawara 1: Voices shouting from the ogre tiles	38
56.	Snowdrop: Snow on the verge	38
57.	Vreemde Bloem: A chalice filled with holy drink	38
58.	Osman Flower: Flower of the house	39
59.	鮎 Ayu: Sat on a rock by a stream	39
60.	Almond Blossom: As I told you, I'm naming him for you	39
61.	Silver Birch 1: A grove of tall white trees	40
62.	Silver Birch 2: My child, she said, a poet be	40
63.	Kaguyabina: I walked through the waving wood	40
64.	藍・紅花 Ai & Benibana: In the soft waters of the north	41
65.	Kōnosu Hinamatsuri: The camera takes the eye to the top	41
66.	Wulai 1: Crimson pink	41
67.	Anemone 1: Gathered in the linen apron	42
68.	Anemone 2: A nodding head I doze	42
69.	Anemone 3: Flower sprung from the blood	42

70.	桜木花道 Sakuragi Hanamichi: Sakuragi you run with the ball	43
71.	Wulai 2: Out of the white cloud	43
72.	貸泉 Kasen: Under the Awaji earth	43
73.	Lambs: Rokkō Pasture the lambs are born	44
74.	二月堂 Nigatsudō: Why within my mind I shout	44
75.	阪急電車 Hankyu Train: Soundlessly the doors open	44
76.	Namaqualand: I got out of the 4x4 and strolled around	45
77.	Rollin': You goin' on a long waltz brother	45
78.	Peace Hana 1: You know I said we have to do something	45
79.	Kanpai: Clouds boil above the hot mash	46
80.	Peace Hana 2: They come from different sides	46
81.	Dame's Rocket: Pale violet cruciform	46
82.	沼島 Nushima: It was when the water was all stirred	47
83.	運慶 Unkei: Within the cypress block	47
84.	豆腐 Tōfu: How many beans in that tub	47
85.	Inflorescence: Clever capitulum	48
86.	Lenten Rose: Found in the Swiss Alps	48
87.	Atsumori: Under the cherry blossom	48
88.	Flower Compassion: I visited them in my thought wishing	49
89.	浪花 Naniwa: Thirty five cards with names	49
90.	Lignite: Forests grew and fell for aeons	49
91.	Flower Fuji 1: The eye of dawn rests on the top	50
92.	Flower Fuji 2: Flower Fuji	50
93.	Akashi Bridge: To the limit of the possible	50
94.	山高神代桜 1: Encoiled in the ancient cherry	51
95.	山高神代桜 2: Homeward from exile	51
96.	Ise Jingu: Light on the mighty roof	51
97.	都おどり Miyako Odori 1: Along the Kamo	52
98.	都おどり Miyako Odori 2: The dancers together turn	52
99.	Buddagaya: In this form tho' unexpected	52
100.	Vision: Whose name is all-compassion	53
101.	灯台躑躅 Dōdan-tsutsuji: Within the tiny umbels	53
102.	Tsubaki Jinja: As I washed my hands I saw	53
103.	Word Flower 3: The cloudless dawn a gift of heaven	54
104.	Cowslip: Level on my own propulsion	54
105.	Cowslip Wine: All of us early that morning ran down to the field	54
106.	Marsh Marigold: The horses had passed through	55
107.	Fragrance Contest: An orchard of flowering trees	55

108.	Nha Nhac: August the drum rolls		55
109.	Red Pepper 1: The lobes of the red pepper		56
110.	Allium: Scrubbed it with a brillo		56
111.	Flower Japan: Time given a world grows		56
112.	Peony: Lions dancing about the peonies		57
113.	美華 Bi Hana: The flower tells the truth		57
114.	Origami Hana: A red square of paper		57
115.	扇子 Fan 1: Round in an arc on a breeze		58
116.	羽衣 Hagoromo: Art is a holy speaking		58
117.	The Flower: The support		58
118.	Three Roses: We released the roots		59
119.	Dance Dragon: Nine bodies make one body		59
120.	Seed: The air is filled with whirring		59
121.	Angelica Tree: Large panicles creamy green-white		60
122.	紫蘭 Shiran: Unwrapped the present		60
123.	Prayer: You'll walk along the file		60
124.	二人静 Futarishizuka: She danced under the cherries		61
125.	小手毬 Kodemari: The hooves pound the track		61
126.	Kindergarten: Parents' day at the kindergarten		61
127.	鈴蘭 Suzuran 1: Look how the green sheaths		62
128.	鈴蘭 Suzuran 2: Prepare a tincture from the root		62
129.	田植え Rice Planting 1: Put the seedlings in the planter		62
130.	Meganebashi: Sing a loud song and merry		63
131.	Kosode Koshimaki 1: White kosode undergarment		63
132.	Peacock: Peacock on a blackthorn		63
133.	猿之助 Ennosuke: I was born to fly		64
134.	田植え Rice Planting 2: Bright green overgrown carpet		64
135.	Water Buffalo: I saw you		64
136.	Speak: The word is love		65
137.	Glimpse: Blue-eyed grass in the meadow		65
138.	Fringed Orchid: Ornaments of lace		65
139.	Bunraku Flower: Stillness in the art		66
140.	辰鼓楼 Shinkorō: Great-grandfather grandpa		66
141.	菖蒲 Shōbu: Sweet smelling reeds on the eaves		66
142.	Kaleidos: Mirror with ten thousand flowers		67
143.	北齋 Hokusai: Butterfly flit by a poppy		67
144.	Lekking: Whinnying at the moorland edge		67
145.	On an Isle: On an island sheltered by trees		68

146.	一輪草	Ichirinsō: The bones of the earth	68
147.		Of a Thousand: The pistils & stamens	68
148.		Lilac Tree 1: Lilac Lilac	69
149.		Word Flower 4: A girl tells me her heart	69
150.		Van Gogh: Closely massed together	69
151.	野苺	Noichigo: I will tell you a secret	70
152.	百合の木	Yurinoki: Pioneer in the eastern woods	70
153.		Silver Birch 3: The slender white runners go before	70
154.		Lilac Tree 2: A flower I took from the lilac tree	71
155.		Red Pepper 2: Whew she was a red hot sizzler	71
156.	つわぶき	Tsuwabuki: Shiny one side hair on the other	71
157.	凌霄花	Nōzenkazura: What her brush makes	72
158.		Hana Ganjin: The grandson of Emperor Temmu	72
159.	紫陽花	Ajisai 1: Walking down the old road	72
160.	黒松	Kuromatsu 2: The garden is a gift of creation	73
161.		Puzzle 1: Flowers in June	73
162.		Time Festival: Carrying clocks the maidens come	73
163.	河童	Kappa: The boy ran over the bridge yelling	74
164.		Black Pepper: Wire mesh around poles	74
165.		Juneberry: Thy gentle finger shows me the fruit	74
166.	소나무	Sonamu: Considering the russet browns	75
167.	叡山電車	Eizandensha: The trolley on the wire sings	75
168.	夏椿	Summer Tsubaki 1: The globe rounding	75
169.		Poplar: Under the pleasant trees	76
170.	夏椿	Summer Tsubaki 2: My flower gone in a day	76
171.	三徳山	Mitoku Mountain: Through the red gate into the woods	76
172.		Myrtle: Take a myrtle wreath	77
173.	鳳凰	Fènghuáng: From out of the West you flew	77
174.		Crape Myrtle 1: Pursued by Ovid you became a tree	77
175.	姫早百合	Himesayuri: Early to blossom princess	78
176.		Tree by Water: Gracefully the slender branches touch the water	78
177.	仁淀川	Niyodogawa: Rain on the height	78
178.	枇杷	Biwa: Loquacious fruit saying	79
179.		Begonias: Not supposed to have a favorite	79
180.		Pupa: Within these quiet walls	79
181.		Lily: Long white trumpet	80
182.		Kuchiko: On the taut string the moist orange	80
183.	千鳥	Chidori 1: Keen a flowering love you sing	80

184.	Papillons: Chimney sweepers in black crepe	81
185.	Ta'amia: Grind the chick peas to a pulp	81
186.	Fynbos: There had been a burn the year before	81
187.	鱧 Hamo: Awaji brought the eel to Yasaka	82
188.	千鳥 Chidori 2: Let the barrel be a bird	82
189.	Mulberry: The weight of the ripe mulberry	82
190.	Hayabusa: Run a circle round the sun	83
191.	Pearl: A perfect word spoken	83
192.	吉祥草 Kichijōsō 1: Still in the black earth	83
193.	Great Purple 1: Through school stages I go	84
194.	Karasu-uri 1: The sap capillaries	84
195.	Frogmore Gardens: In prayer walking the graceful lawn	84
196.	Snowy Egret: Walking in the uplands	85
197.	Bougainvillea: A vine of purple bracts	85
198.	Jet: Flaps. Thrust. Pitch the nose up	85
199.	Gion Festival: Tower high on great wheels	86
200.	Trees: The oak in the field is a round hat	86
201.	Phosphoresce: Little spirits	86
202.	山百合 Yamayuri 1: Of my love for thee	87
203.	山百合 Yamayuri 2: Not a wand but an armful	87
204.	山百合 Yamayuri 3: She will stand still most silent	87
205.	Kirin 1: Pardon me your Highness	88
206.	Kirin 2: Gobi Bactrian	88
207.	Kirin 3: Though you don't belong	88
208.	Mugunghwa 1: What names are given	89
209.	Mugunghwa 2: Methanol extract	89
210.	Mugunghwa 3: Round white sails	89
211.	西瓜 Suika 1: Look at the fluff	90
212.	西瓜 Suika 2: Chiganemaru thy blade	90
213.	西瓜 Suika 3: Bright thy face arise today	90
214.	栄螺 Sazae 1: Comes everything	91
215.	Kitano Tenmangu Festival: We found ourselves in the shrine	91
216.	Oud: The prince bowed in greeting	91
217.	Mountain Spring: Heart in the cold airs	92
218.	Flag: Golden dove with soaring wings	92
219.	飴細工 Amezaiku: Up the slope past the festival booths	92
220.	Globe & Streamers: They dance in the happy breeze	93
221.	Identifying: The other side of the room	93

222.	Peace Flower: Gather them from here & there	93
223.	Time Square: They were dancing in the square	94
224.	Hoverflies: Striped like a wasp & wafer-thin	94
225.	Manga Flower: Through the portals of imagination	94
226.	Cacao Pod 1: Held in my hand	95
227.	Cacao Pod 2: A green and golden pod	95
228.	千年 Thousand Years: They gave the kids a project	95
229.	父ちゃん Totchan: Small wee voice shouting	96
230.	大山 Daisen: A carton of milk	96
231.	Tobacco: Open the memory sachet	96
232.	Ainu Flower 1: Voices rise and fall around we go	97
233.	Ainu Flower 2: The women hammer out the chant	97
234.	Ainu Flower 3: In winter the sea will freeze white	97
235.	真名井滝 Manai Waterfall: Alone I flew from the high bridge	98
236.	愛の輪 Ainowa: Youngsters with various challenges	98
237.	Matsuage Festival: Basket on the top of the pole	98
238.	Cloudman: Potter with a lump of white	99
239.	Waxflower: These were the seals	99
240.	晒菜升麻 Sarashina Shōma: You stink in my nose	99
241.	鬼瓦 Onigawara 2: Don't you remember? We were 12	100
242.	Faith Flower: Allies in the struggle	100
243.	栄螺 Sazae 2: The round pail above me	100
244.	Drums: Talk talk says the Noh drum	101
245.	杜鵑草 Unnamed: Utterly I refuse to tell them your name	101
246.	Crowberry: The heather drowses	101
247.	台湾杜鵑草 Taiwan Hototogisu: Blush mauve	102
248.	椎茸 Shiitake: Sit beside the log	102
249.	Fishing Boats: Blue-green the sea-surface slides	102
250.	Hokkaido: Small knobbly earth-fruits	103
251.	Brugsmansia: All was quiet in the large hall	103
252.	Phenom: The engines whistle up	103
253.	榎 Enoki 1: Planted on highways	104
254.	Fig 1: Fig pollination	104
255.	Night Fishing: The engine rumbles, bangs and groans	104
256.	Stormgods 1: The roof goes from east to west	105
257.	Stormgods 2: Oho aha the mighty drums	105
258.	Stormgods 3: Oooh aaah the sac is opened	105
259.	新幹線 Shinkansen: Smooth white alabaster thy aero body	106

260.	Fig 2: This little life	106
261.	Harvest: The fields were golden	106
262.	竹 Bamboo 1: Walk through the bamboo forest	107
263.	竹 Bamboo 2: Forest of green bamboo	107
264.	竹 Bamboo 3: Seasoned in the weather	107
265.	White Dove: There's a princess with doves	108
266.	Rushes: Strewn on the hard floor	108
267.	Crab Apple: Jam jars on the white tiles	108
268.	Ebisu 1: Under your arm a golden bream	109
269.	Ebisu 2: Get Ebisu from the super	109
270.	Islands: On the horizon	109
271.	興福寺三重塔 Kōfukuji: Built to hold his holy bones	110
272.	ゆ Yu: On the cool north side of the hills	110
273.	藤袴 Fujibakama: In the small white pot	110
274.	生花 Ikebana 1: Stare at the artwork	111
275.	生花 Ikebana 2: To tell you the perfection of the flower	111
276.	生花 Ikebana 3: By flower arrangement	111
277.	生花 Ikebana 4: I assembled a panoply of smell	112
278.	檜扇 Hiōgi: The leaves hide her secret smile	112
279.	鴨上戸 Hiyodori Jōgo: A tangle of autumn vines and leaf	112
280.	Mube: Purple potatoes hanging in the air	113
281.	円椎 Tsuburajii: I gathered you as treasure	113
282.	岩蓮華 Iwarenge: Modest in my hope	113
283.	Citron: Green capsule turn yellow	114
284.	Abundance: The leaves are golden	114
285.	Wind: The fude lightly touches the paper	114
286.	Harvesters 1: Handles like a dream	115
287.	Harvesters 2: The whole village	115
288.	Harvesters 3: Specks in the eye	115
289.	Ginkgo 1: Eighteen thousand yellow flags	116
290.	Ginkgo 2: The leaf is printed on a stone tablet	116
291.	Ginkgo 3: Though the cliff crumble beneath me	116
292.	山黄櫨 Yamahaze: Coppery-bronze spear blades	117
293.	Sumac: Dried and crushed	117
294.	Japan Flower 1: What am I to thee?	117
295.	Japan Flower 2: Shall we go back in time	118
296.	傘寿 Sanju: Stairs go up behind you	118
297.	薄 Susuki: A black lacquered box	118

13

298.	荻 Ogi: The old man's hair and beard	119
299.	Fuji Ringo: Slender white fingers I admired	119
300.	Akashiyaki: A golden globe	119
301.	Autumn Maple: The first frost gripped my ankles hard	120
302.	Autumn Cherry: The leaves of the cherry turn autumn	120
303.	万作 Mansaku: A clown with a paper streamer	120
304.	Tororo: Long pale brown hairy limb	121
305.	踊り Odori: Observe the precision of the fingers	121
306.	Mozuku: How the sweet chestnut	121
307.	Kaede Momiji 1: They put scalding lights under the maples	122
308.	Kaede Momiji 2: Sunset flung her robes upon the trees	122
309.	Kaede Momiji 3: Calling on myself for inspiration	122
310.	Kaede Momiji 4: How cold it is this morning	123
311.	橅 Buna: The wind polished the sky	123
312.	小菊 Kogiku: A field of yellow flowers	123
313.	吉祥草 Kichijōsō 2: Planted in the garden to bring joy	124
314.	Takeda Castle: It is cold at dawn in the eyrie	124
315.	Satsumaimo: Bright minerals Kirishima	124
316.	Coffee 2: A wicker basket of ripe coffee beans	125
317.	言葉 Palavras: Jingle joyfully I ring the bell	125
318.	Karasu-uri 2: Galaxies without number	125
319.	Japanese Maple: The names make a poem	126
320.	Akashi Nori: Pulling on the red net roller	126
321.	Kosode Koshimaki 2: Ask me the meaning	126
322.	Single Malt: Pale gold amber	127
323.	Nori Seaweed: Haul the nets from the Inland sea	127
324.	Sushi: My eyes follow the rapid folding	127
325.	菊の花 Kiku no Hana: A jar of water	128
326.	秋明菊 Shūmeigiku: Spotlight from the cloud a hold	128
327.	Taylor: With one look you apprise him	128
328.	榎 Enoki 2: The tree grew peacefully in the forest	129
329.	和紙 Washi: Pasha! Pasha!	129
330.	Akashi Tako Senbei: Old red baldy boiled soft	129
331.	舞踏 Butoh: Learn wisdom	130
332.	Ballet Flower: Will no one dance it properly	130
333.	沖ノ島 Okinoshima 2: Early days in a good wind	130
334.	Crab: 蟹 life you are giving	131
335.	町家 Machiya: Old road in the Kobe hills	131

336.		Aurora 1: The air was dry & completely clear	131
337.		Winter Jasmine 2: On the trellis dark green shoots	132
338.		Rice Bowl: steam 息	132
339.		First Ones: Tribal conflict drove us eastwards	132
340.	福玉	Fukudama: Hemispheres of rice	133
341.	海老蔵	Ebizō: The family business is art	133
342.		Encourager: Boldly she spoke	133
343.	養命酒	Yōmeishu 1: A tonic to restore me, to raise the life in me	134
344.	養命酒	Yōmeishu 2: Second dose of tonic with epimedium	134
345.	養命酒	Yōmeishu 3: Du Zhong to calm me	134
346.		Puzzle 2: Struck the head against the black	135
347.	芝翫	Shikan: High voice sings in the nose	135
348.		Aurora 2: In the arctic sky	135
349.		Puzzle 3: Shall I follow a star on lovely wings	136
350.		Hot Sake: As the warmth moved through me	136
351.	湯たんぽ	Yutanpo: I find an old friend	136
352.	備前	Bizen: How the light runs along the blade	137
353.	広辞苑	Kōjien: Looking for a friend	137
354.		Teacher: Help me to understand	137
355.		Brahms Flower: Time beside us calls the dance to end	138
356.		Hot Water Bottle: Old rubber belly	138
357.		Solstice: Druids cut the mistle from the oak	138
358.		Happy Birthday: Majestic dragon on a gold coin	139
359.		Gratitude: The charities came to lunch in the Mall	139
360.	猿	Saru 1: Red-faced	139
361.	猿	Saru 2: It is Christmas time	140
362.	猿	Saru 3: The forests have all but gone	140
363.		Celebration: Great swollen bladders	140
364.		Peace Maker: A time for honeyed odes to lift up praise	141
365.		Skytree Tokyo: Arm in arm	141
366.	花火	Hanabi: The children cried out with high voices	141
367.		Epilogue Poem: 華 Hana	142

Notes on the Poems	145
Profile	155
Author's Profits	156
Books by Stean Anthony	157

16

Preface

This is an anthology of short poems on the theme of flowers arranged as a calendar. It is a companion volume to *Bird* and to *Sport*, both collections published by Yamaguchi. I have interpreted the concept of flower freely, and I have also included many poems which strictly speaking do not belong here. You will find many poems which are linked to Japan, and I also use Japanese kanji quite often. I do so for aesthetic reasons. You can find brief explanations in the notes at the end of the book.

This volume is intended as book of celebration and of gratitude. Although I have no merit or ability, and without any formal action, it is privately offered to the sovereigns of both Japan and of the United Kingdom, His Majesty Emperor Akihito and Her Majesty Queen Elizabeth II. I wish to say thank you to them, conscious of so many good things they have achieved for world peace, and for the strength they have shown in their duty.

Books consulted
Kōgō Michiko sama no Miuta [Empress Michiko's Verse]. Tokyo: PIE International, 2015.
Michiko sama [Empress of Japan]. *100 no Kotoba* [One Hundred Words]. Tokyo: Takarajimasha, 2016.
I have responded to some select verses by Empress Michiko [abbreviated EM]. As is well known in Japan, she is an accomplished poet.

Websites consulted
http://www.hana300.com/
http://botanyboy.org/

I have consulted a wide range of websites, too many to mention. For any errors of fact or information I am solely responsible. There is no intention in this book to cause offense. This is a book of thanksgiving and celebration.

Acknowledgements
I am grateful for the support of my publisher, especially HT for her great help, and also KM for her kindness and diligence.

Preface Poem:　華　Hana

If I count thy lines what shall I find
A pattern to number the clouds
Or a ladder in Eden
Spirits by thee descend to earth
From thee to me breathes Heaven.

If I rest my eye upon you
Where will I be
At the fountain of joy again
Safe at last where I long to be
Under thy heart happy at peace again.

If my nose can comprehend thee
Let me sing this song
How many lines of fragrant joy
Her gentle petal against my finger
His perfume so sweet to me I laughed I cried.

20

1   Jan 1   Hanapoem 1
She asked me why
I said
I love you very much
I do
Then I said, won't you?

2   Jan 2   Hanapoem 2
I'm drawing pictures to say
Dear friend
What I cannot say
Another way
Look up there love a flower!

3   Jan 3   Hanapoem 3
Born on a flower
Life is a fiction
Why live in this harsh world
As if it were real
It has been a flower the whole way.

4   Jan 4   火花   Hibana
Tumbles from the quarry wall
The stone strikes the shovel edge
It splits perfectly in two
Blue-black depths
A spark leapt across.

5   Jan 5   Anthesis
The fingers flicker through the light
A thousand galaxies in flower
A million suns like pollen
Through the air
In one instant the glory of creation.

6   Jan 6   Karuta
Cut me up & spread me on the floor
Calling in high voices
Seize me
Bright in Heian raiment
Now put me together for another year.

22

7   Jan 7   七草   Nanakusa 1
On the seventh day of January
Being Christmas in Moscow
Blessings in Japan
A gentle bowl of nanakusa
Boiled rice with seven green herbs.

8   Jan 8   七草   Nanakusa 2
Seri 芹 green vigor
Nazuna 薺 an ornament
Tiny white flowers
The seedpod a green heart
Hotokenoza 仏座 what do you say?

9   Jan 9   七草   Nanakusa 3
The throne of charity
The loving heart
The one of pity
Serene sky above the hills
The teacher who gives wisdom.

23

10   Jan 10   七草   Nanakusa 4
Suzuna 菘 the white cloud
Suzushiro 蘿蔔 the soul of health
Hakobe 繁縷 the heart of mercy
Gogyō 御形 the hand that gives
Japan be born & hold us safe this year.

11   Jan 11   櫻   Cherry
Mother gathered clams in the shallow water
She was there in the sea when the sun rose
As beautiful as the cherry blossom in spring
She sang as she worked, to thee I say thank you
You have given us food and kept us safe once again.

12   Jan 12   Asahi
I found an old poster
In her hand a bottle of Asahi
On the label the rays of the rising sun
In art I find a way to love
Who shall you be?

24

13 Jan 13   黒松   Kuromatsu 1

The black pine on the white sand
The sunlight in the pine needles gold
The movement in the branches
The change in direction
The garden is art.

14 Jan 14   沖ノ島   Okinoshima 1

Holy dwelling of the guardian
Invisible from the sea arise
Defend us holy one
In the peace
The wood echoes my prayers.

15 Jan 15   Almond

To greet the year in bridal white
The blossom after winter rain
More bright
The slopes of Carmel
The heart alive to the beauty of Creation.

16　Jan 16　Family Flower
Observe the bud
The linen of the petal
Neatly unfolds
Life pushes thru
Arms wide open welcome home!

17　Jan 17　翡翠　Hisui
In the formation of the land
The earth plates ran together
Molten rock with mineral salts
Where the river runs a thread
White jade glimmers light green.

18　Jan 18　玄米茶　Genmaicha
A tablespoon of light amber oil
Steamed brown rice
Roast in the pan till the rice jumps
An equal quantity of green tea
Pour on boiling water let it stand.

19   Jan 19   Bell Pepper

Looking at the bells
Golden yellow
Glossy cactus green
Red so bold
So good I love you.

20   Jan 20   Cockerel

White bantam with the scarlet wattle
    Strutting in the yard
        Watching every move
            Life in this good earth
Defend it! I'm shouting   watch yer step!

21   Jan 21   Mustard Chicken

In the hot olive oil
A handful of seeds
They leap and shout
Put in chicken pieces & soy
Stir in pepper, olives, honey & figs.

22   Jan 22   絵島   Eshima

Cloudless night without wind
Stand on this rock
Plovers cry
The moon in the waves
The bridge leaps and hums.

23   Jan 23   Kuromame

Tangled bean vines heaped on rice poles
The morning dew, the breezes blow
The sun dries, the pods brown
天道様 Old Father Sun
Thy gift the bright black bean.

24   Jan 24   Bourne by the Waves

Great islands sail upon the water
Little children dance upon the shore
In a storm the wild waters foam
In a calm with mother
On the sand we gather the sea green health.

28

25   Jan 25   牡丹鍋   Botan Nabe

Shall I be the beaters
Driving him to the nets
Or shall I run with him
Hurtling through the forest
Ending on a plate a petalled rose?

26   Jan 26   豆乳   Tōnyū

Still warm in the sealware beaker
On my way to the train
I drink the milk
Coins in the basket
Window seat on the green velvet.

27   Jan 27   Tago no Ura

Walking along the shore
Gazing on Mount Fuji
Pure white on the summit
Akahito stand with me
Help me to say.

28   Jan 28   Garlic Leaf
Harvest the green leaves at dawn
The chill prevents spoiling
Chopped and ground
Bright green zing
Tai sashimi.

29   Jan 29   Kimono Flower
Japonica printed on cream silk
Blue-grey inner kimono
Gold chrys on black obi
Rainbow shimmers
On the petal the velvet pin.

30   Jan 30   笠取山   Kasatori 1
From the heights of Kasatori
The forest clothes the land
From the rock where I stand
The water starts to flow
A blessing word a rivulet & stream.

30

31 Jan 31   笠取山 Kasatori 2

From the heights of Kasatori
The gaze rests on white lace
Clarity floats in the distance
Her hands release waters
The rivers and the city fountains.

32 Feb 1   Era Name 1

The man held up the white sign
平成 the new era name
Peace-making
Name to say our hope
For others to know the way we go.

33 Feb 2   節分 Setsubun

Start the seasons turning
A priest to ward off badness
He wore both robes by heaven
He threw the beans and shouts
Fortune and happiness be in Japan.

34   Feb 3   Yamata no Orochi 1
Our ancient dreams alive before us
The hero and the demons
The great coiling earth snake
The Prince in his virtue makes us safe
The white robed priest shouts a word of joy!

35   Feb 4   Yamata no Orochi 2
Eight wooden vats of perfumed wine
Trembling they wait
Slithers an earthquake a land moving
The eight heads drink and sleep
The Prince strikes and lo! The shining sword!

36   Feb 5   Yamata no Orochi 3
Out of the sky realms bright-robed
Who should you be but my guardian
By the river I stood weeping and praying
Out of the sunlight you stand
Now the snake is dead and I am saved.

32

37   Feb 6   Era Name 2
The new name to follow tradition
To change tradition
To serve
What should it be
How can we say *love thy neighbor?*

38   Feb 7   Era Name 3
That was the meaning of Heisei
It was a holy verse
For you and me
Let us say it again
Warmer & brighter the same prayer.

39   Feb 8   Spring Herbs
Mother Mãe gather herbs for family
Gather them in your basket
Prepare the herbal tea
Together sipping
Praying together bless us Mother.

40   Feb 9   Flower Poetry
Take a deep breath
Breathe in
Poet walk back
To the founts of verse
Flow the water with thy pen.

41   Feb 10   Winter Jasmine 1
From my green sleeve my hand
In a red glove
Now I open my fist
Flew a dove from my hat
It's a yellow headwrap bright sun.

42   Feb 11   Kobe Waterfall
The heat fled to the sky
Winter cast her net
Glittering lace
Spring will be soon
Let the water sing above Kobe.

34

43   Feb 12   Hasedera Festival 1

Brightly burn the fiery torch
Round the wooden house
Roaring uu ōō
Clap cymbals blow conch
Family our sins be forgiven.

44   Feb 13   Coffee 1

Highland spring abundant flowers
The brides are in white
Gorgeous they stand
Shivering with the thought
The bridegrooms stand at the door.

45   Feb 14   源信   Genshin

Great father with a flower soul
1000 years fled like a day
You taught us truth
Not by self but by Thee
To rise to the pure land of bliss.

46   Feb 15   Plum Blossom

Is there snow on the wall in the Kyoto garden
I'd go back there again this moment
Take my hand
I would say
I'd stay there and say again what I said.

47   Feb 16   Hasedera Festival 2

By the power of the word
Defeat our dark
The flame
Purify remember
1000 years a happy marriage.

48   Feb 17   Heart Flower

Weather chart Japan is bright sun
Festival in Okayama
Ten thousand naked bodies
Happy mothers' sons
Love bonds us as we strive to win.

36

49   Feb 18   Kairakuen
Snow-white tabi on the goza
The blossom on the trees
Spring in Mito
The girls wear white kimono
Petalled hands are dancing.

50   Feb 19   Prunus
Absolutely gorgeous
Exquisite blossom
Just perfect
Tell me now
What d'ya have to do?

51   Feb 20   Winter Daphne
A heady musk
I turned to look
Princess FF
The leaves shining
Her perfume all-conquering.

37

52   Feb 21   お守り   Omamori
He came to Brazil on the first boat
One hundred years ago
Heart-strings sang a song of home
Look at his mamori
Silk-bright say long root remember.

53   Feb 22   Word Flower 1
To be as I ought
Stretched to my limit
My heart turned red
Red of the banner
Gentle and kind.

54   Feb 23   Word Flower 2
Looking to an island
We depend on each other
Service our life and thought
My life steeped in duty
Child of my family.

55   Feb 24   鬼瓦   Onigawara 1
Voices shouting from the ogre tiles
Blithering stupid blasted fool
What me?   YOU!   Dim-witted
Ease-loving shallow-cultured
Don't-read no-knowledge modern fool!

56   Feb 25   Snowdrop
Snow on the verge
Under the tall yew hedge
It was dry. Her head bowed
In a prayer of love
Her face pale as a snowdrop in spring.

57   Feb 26   Vreemde Bloem
A chalice filled with holy drink
It was so vibrantly bright
Authority shone
Is there not a power here
We became jealous and secret.

58   Feb 27   Osman Flower
Flower of the house
I wore it in my hat
The name from that
I wrote the true name
I sang it in my prayer.

Peace flower with Islam! الله

59   Feb 28   鮎   Ayu
Sat on a rock by a stream
Counting
The ayu leap through the spray
They climb to the heights
Carry my prayer *help defend the rivers!*

60   Feb 29   Almond Blossom
As I told you, I'm naming him for you
May he be as stubborn & brave
May God bless the boy
All my love to you   Theo
Read the work as a map.

61   March 1   Silver Birch 1
A grove of tall white trees
Leaves like hands shake the breeze
Who is the woman half-glimpsed
An Elven Queen
Smiling on me with a blessing given?

62   March 2   Silver Birch 2
My child, she said, a poet be
She took the leaf of the goodly tree
A diamond verse that trembles
A golden song to sing
A silver line she gave to me.

63   March 3   Kaguyabina
I walked through the waving wood
Tall columns talking together
Turning around a column
I saw a prince and his bride
In a golden room they wore flowers.

64   March 4   藍・紅花   Ai & Benibana
In the soft waters of the north
Steeping the raw silk
A twist of thread
Beni and Ai   flower and root
You shall make the cloth for my table.

65   March 5   Kōnosu Hinamatsuri
The camera takes the eye to the top
There are too many to count
I am reminded
Both here & there the perfect
Our hope in them struggles onward.

66   March 6   Wulai 1
Crimson pink
Azalea cherries
A line in the air
Can I look away
As the waterfall roars applause.

42

67   March 7   Anemone 1
Gathered in the linen apron
Petals for the offering
Be gentle with me
Brightness of my hope
May the girl I love return my longing.

68   March 8   Anemone 2
A nodding head I doze
In the sun I stand
Open eyes awake
Star on the woodland floor
I doze again when the sun goes in.

69   March 9   Anemone 3
Flower sprung from the blood
Flower bloom with a wind
Pearl on the petal roll
Water the earth by the tree
Spring from the earth alive anew.

43

70   March 10   桜木花道   Sakuragi Hanamichi

Sakuragi you run with the ball
A garden in spring
Through the blossoms you breeze
A day of sun
Well played!   your beloved you won.

71   March 11   Wulai 2

Out of the white cloud
A line of thunder
Splashing
The fine mist
Carries the sweet fragrance.

72   March 12   貸泉   Kasen

Under the Awaji earth
A brown coin
An old five yen
Date to the late Han
Good news from far away.

44

73   March 13   Lambs

Rokkō Pasture the lambs are born
There's a shot a few days old
His ears are pinkish white
Looks happy with his mother
She is serene the first chapters of life.

74   March 14   二月堂   Nigatsudō

Why within my mind I shout
A bell with a blurred tongue
Through the body expended
Burn from me my selfishness
The fire runs around the chant high.

75   March 15   阪急電車   Hankyu Train

Soundlessly the doors open
Green plush velvet
At your service
Smoothly the wheels glide
Kyoto dawn sun rise joy to Osaka.

76   March 16   Namaqualand
I got out of the 4x4 and strolled around
A field of daisies in a heaven riot
I walk with my companion
In a dream together
Happy in the garden will there be no fall.

77   March 17   Rollin'
You goin' on a long waltz brother
Flower over land & under sea
Up there in harvest time
Here on my finger
Did I tell you I gotten real happy?

78   March 18   Peace Hana 1
You know I said we have to do something
That it makes no sense talking about peace
Unless we actually do something
Well look what I found
They sang and folded cranes together.

79   March 19   Kanpai
Clouds boil above the hot mash
The waters surge and seethe
Releasing words
The pure liquor fills the cup
The level at my eye I see the sky.

80   March 20   Peace Hana 2
They come from different sides
Folding a crane together
What does it mean
Life and health
Turk & Greek sing in Japanese.

81   March 21   Dame's Rocket
Pale violet cruciform
A bee plunges in
Moment then
She's gone
The petals bounce.

82   March 22   沼島   Nushima

It was when the water was all stirred
The deep earth erupted up
Folded over and kneaded
The waters all the while foaming
Rushing and swirling with a great noise.

83   March 23   運慶   Unkei

Within the cypress block
The house upheld
Patiently
The disguise
I have taken away.

84   March 24   豆腐   Tōfu

How many beans in that tub
Name me each one
Through the muslin
The milk I grew on
Pure white unbroken hope Japan.

48

85   March 25   Inflorescence
Clever capitulum
Sorting in a flash
Raceme & umbel
Panicle & cyme
Corymb & spike.

86   March 26   Lenten Rose
Found in the Swiss Alps
Flowers as the snow melts
The petals do not fall
The follicle swells
Black seeds the warm earth.

87   March 27   Atsumori
Under the cherry blossom
A young man not yet twenty
Pale brow translucent fair
His eyes closed his lips pursed
A flute breathing an old song.

88   March 28   Flower Compassion
I visited them in my thought wishing
To leap constraints and tell them
My heart cried out to them
Feeling their suffering
What can I give what can I do for you.

89   March 29   浪花   Naniwa
Thirty five cards with names
In his hands he held them
He prayed for each
One will build the church
His grandchild prays there today.

90   March 30   Lignite
Forests grew and fell for aeons
Laid to sleep under heavy blankets
Millions of years they rested in peace
The digger loads them into the truck
They disappear in a flicker of flame.

91   March 31   Flower Fuji 1
The eye of dawn rests on the top
The clouds run lengthwise
Through the skies
Many years thy many years
The sun set glorious sun rise here.

92   April 1   Flower Fuji 2
Flower Fuji
Mountain of beauty
Ineffable goodness
Mother mountain
Flower life.

93   April 2   Akashi Bridge
To the limit of the possible
Timing and connection
Regard the silhouette
Our record in safety
Read the bridge a word of joy.

94　April 3　山高神代桜 1

Encoiled in the ancient cherry
A flameless fire within
White blossom like snow
The hollow trunk is a throne
Love sits there love sings my song.

95　April 4　山高神代桜 2

Homeward from exile
The long road walked
Gift of the true heart
Be thanks for this grace
Love will find life in this flowering.

96　April 5　Ise Jingu

Light on the mighty roof
Raised above the earth
The land we love
Heaven within
Our love for one another.

52

97   April 6   都おどり   Miyako Odori 1

Along the Kamo
The cherries started to bloom
To the happy strum of the shamisen
Their white feet point and turn
The petals dancing.

98   April 7   都おどり   Miyako Odori 2

The dancers together turn
What can art achieve
Order in beauty
The fan opens in joy
華やか   the fabric folds.

99   April 8   Buddagaya

In this form tho' unexpected
In my life I return
Flow back to the flowering
Strength renewing in the chant
Calling the true unchanging peace.

100   April 9   Vision
Whose name is all-compassion
With his legs folded and soles upward
He is freedom from the suffering world
The angels around him in joyful concert
Dulcet harmony on the ancient lute.

101   April 10   灯台躑躅   Dōdan-tsutsuji
Within the tiny umbels
Dwell the ancient spirits
Guardians of the woodland
They make themselves small
And sing in the dancing breeze.

102   April 11   Tsubaki Jinja
As I washed my hands I saw
Reflected in the water
A bright red face with long nose
A beard and a spear
He laughed at me   a bright smile.

103   April 12   Word Flower 3
The cloudless dawn a gift of heaven
My spirit bright and true
To choose the pure
Water in the air
Let me hold thee my whole life thru.

104   April 13   Cowslip
Level on my own propulsion
A sweet scent at the golden mouth
I reach deep within the pouch
Drinking the sweetness
Power to my wings and body flows.

105   April 14   Cowslip Wine
All of us early that morning ran down to the field
The world rang with birdsong as we gathered
Only the long stalks with plentiful bells
Soon the baskets were filled
Back at the farm we sorted the sweet-smelling peeps.

106   April 15   Marsh Marigold
The horses had passed through
There were small puddles
Shapes of cloud & sky
Undaunted beside
A yellow gleam in the black mud.

107   April 16   Fragrance Contest
An orchard of flowering trees
You are welcome to try
Tie the blindfold on
Identify each one
Can you hope to win against me?

108   April 17   Nha Nhac
August the drum rolls
The gods assemble
Long & high hold the note
Solemn court musicians
Listen! The hour-glass drum!

109   April 18   Red Pepper 1
The lobes of the red pepper
This makes them great for stuffing
You can put in just about anything
I knew someone adventurous
Feta couscous olives pine-nuts basil.

110   April 19   Allium
Scrubbed it with a brillo
Pounded with a pomice
Poured on pints of bleach
Tried dousing it with whisky
Just could not get rid of the stink.

111   April 20   Flower Japan
Time given a world grows
The letters are learnt
A hand out-held
The lines will flower
Let us love one another & live.

112   April 21   Peony
Lions dancing about the peonies
Shaking their shaggy manes
Flowers open beauty
Flutter the petals in a breeze
Auspicious dance bring in a blessing!

113   April 22   美華   Bi Hana
The flower tells the truth
Within the image is an image
Behind the face another face
Before the wisdom wisdom
Teacher flower now in front of me.

114   April 23   Origami Hana
A red square of paper
Her fingers fold in
Fingers flower
A water lily
She stood radiant with the children.

58

115   April 24   扇子   Fan 1

Round in an arc on a breeze
Lifted up and turned
Held above
Turned upside down
Shall I dance in your hand?

116   April 25   羽衣   Hagoromo

Art is a holy speaking
I have worn the feather robe
Turning my soul in circles
Ascending in steps
Climbing the sky.

117   April 26   The Flower

The support
Five performers
An article of news
Words of high praise
Can I do the same I think.

118   April 27   Three Roses
We released the roots
Placed it gently in the hole
Tamped down the black mulch
Root stock with three green arms
Bloom a red, white and a golden rose.

119   April 28   Dance Dragon
Nine bodies make one body
We follow the 王 uplifted
Smile bright jade dragon
Dance Kobe to Macao
Friendship a victory we win.

120   April 29   Seed
The air is filled with whirring
Writing circles
A wall of wisteria
A garden door
White & purple on left & right.

60

121   April 30   Angelica Tree
Large panicles creamy green-white
August flowers
Green shoots are fragrant in May
Tara or Dure
Same word   a mountain blessing.

122   May 1   紫蘭   Shiran
Unwrapped the present
The land ploughed
Chalky white loam
Streaked with orange
La beneicon de la récolte.

123   May 2   Prayer
You'll walk along the file
Gazed upon by millions
May you stand in the light
Guarded by goodness
Thou be the brightness.

124   May 3   二人静   Futarishizuka
She danced under the cherries
Pictures on her kimono
Coiffed like a fabulous bird
A pink blossom snowfall
I danced   we still dance.

125   May 4   小手毬   Kodemari
The hooves pound the track
The crowd cheer as they pass
Such unstoppable strength
To celebrate, by the stream
The pure white kodemari.

126   May 5   Kindergarten
Parents' day at the kindergarten
The tiny tots dancing
Little hands flower
Look at Mum & Dad
Waving their arms and laughing.

62

127   May 6   鈴蘭   Suzuran 1

Look how the green sheaths
Curl round and funnel
The rain to the flower root
Rising in pure white bells
After rain a lovely scent.

128   May 7   鈴蘭   Suzuran 2

Prepare a tincture from the root
A tonic for my heart
Happy I remember you
See how the pure white bells
Glow in the autumn like coral beads.

129   May 8   田植え   Rice Planting 1

Put the seedlings in the planter
The bony claw
Picks one out and plants it
Poet harvest
Thy page made a perfect suture.

130   May 9   Meganebashi

Sing a loud song and merry
For the engineers
Raise your hat to the Romans
Sakazuki of wine
Toast in honor of the Japanese.

131   May 10   Kosode Koshimaki 1

White kosode undergarment
Quiet within   I wear
Three seasons of color
The fifth layer a blossom
The sixth at my waist is a skirt.

132   May 11   Peacock

Peacock on a blackthorn
Out of the rainbow
Whose eyes
Regard
Life is a sudden flowering.

64

133 May 12 猿之助 Ennosuke

I was born to fly
In the wind of the applause
I rose slowly above the crowd
Smoke billowed as I shouted out
Far below the demons gurned.

134 May 13 田植え Rice Planting 2

Bright green overgrown carpet
How quickly the world can change
When I was born no such machine
Now every field in Japan
Spirit in the rice what does it mean?

135 May 14 Water Buffalo

I saw you
Pulling the city
Patient and strong
You give unrewarded
And then I said angel.

136   May 15   Speak

The word is love
The letter is love
The heart is love
The figure is love
The character is love.

137   May 16   Glimpsed

Blue-eyed grass in the meadow
Winds are never still
The cattails rustle
The laden bees hum
In the flowers blessed Lord you come.

138   May 17   Fringed Orchid

Ornaments of lace
Starched white veils
Her head has wings
Egret feathers
Royal Society for Protection.

66

139   May 18   Bunraku Flower

Stillness in the art
The flicker of an eyelid
The shoulder turned
Humanity
A world of joy and grief.

140   May 19   辰鼓楼   Shinkorō

Great-grandfather grandpa
World changes old man
Here is the good news
The stork is a-wing
On high he says happy land!

141   May 20   菖蒲   Shōbu

Sweet smelling reeds on the eaves
Rushes beneath my pillow
Green sword defend me
Perfume go with me
In the onsen give health.

142   May 21   Kaleidos
Mirror with ten thousand flowers
Pipe ten thousand blooms
My eye to the scope
Thoughts getting thoughts
My heart spins round in changes.

143   May 22   北齋   Hokusai
Butterfly flit by a poppy
Warm heart we live by
Beat the rainy cold
Spring not winter
Mighty red Fuji tower forever.

144   May 23   Lekking
Whinnying at the moorland edge
Dawn now. The grouse fizz
Dancing up and back
Those Scottish primadonnas
Their red wattles and bright sheen.

68

145   May 24   On an Isle

On an island sheltered by trees
I shall sit like the one above
Reading the holy poetry
The heart at peace
The sea speaks softly as I pray.

146   May 25   一輪草   Ichirinsō

The bones of the earth
Remember
The good land is a gift
White flower
Generations lived & died.

147   May 26   Of a Thousand

The pistils & stamens
A thousand ways to help
The body of the people
The body of mercy
Standing still and dancing.

148   May 27   Lilac Tree 1
Lilac Lilac
Hang out your flags
Each one a heart *Lilac Lilac*
At home again sing out in dream
My heart in sun   shine on the tree.

149   May 28   Word Flower 4
A girl tells me her heart
Is it a spear
Or a lance
Or thought to be done
Think about how they feel.

150   May 29   Van Gogh
Closely massed together
There was a troupe of them
Moving as though with the wind
Beautiful otherworldly pale blue faces
Looked at me and beckoned sweetly.

151 May 30 野苺 Noichigo

I will tell you a secret
Only the blackbird knows
Look under the leaves
Sweet and sour
Wild strawberries.

152 May 31 百合の木 Yurinoki

Pioneer in the eastern woods
Warily forward on autumn paths
We stand before a tall yellow glory
The guide says we make canoes
Later we discover the lilies in May.

153 June 1 Silver Birch 3

The slender white runners go before
Loosing clouds of pollen
They held the damp ground
Generations falling and rising
Their sacrifice the space of our life.

154　June 2　Lilac Tree 2

A flower I took from the lilac tree
From the tree beneath my room
Remember a day my heart in glee
Freed from school on a day in June
My world was filled with a sweet perfume.

155　June 3　Red Pepper 2

Whew she was a red hot sizzler
Bit that one and the steam came out my nose
Eyes rolled round and round
The tears flooded out the room
The ears started flapping to cool my toes.

156　June 4　つわぶき　Tsuwabuki

Shiny one side hair on the other
Boil the stems and small leaf
Peel to the lucent core
Boil two minutes
Steep in salt water and serve.

157　June 5　凌霄花　Nōzenkazura

What her brush makes
She is about to sing
How she loved me
Her golden voice
A watercolor of my childhood.

158　June 6　　Hana Ganjin

The grandson of Emperor Temmu
I send one thousand kesa
Tho the land differ
In this kesa the same sky
The world is gone we meet in heaven.

159　June 7　紫陽花　Ajisai 1

Walking down the old road
Shaking the earth from your feet
Rattling leaves and blossoms
It's a long way old friend
Here you are in my life bright Japan.

73

160   June 8   黒松   Kuromatsu 2
The garden is a gift of creation
Kneel on the sand by the pine
Silently take the fragrance
No more than a whisper
In the moist sunlit air.

161   June 9   Puzzle 1
Flowers in June
Before the monsoon
When the green turns red
Dry the red in the sun
Black will turn gold.

162   June 10   Time Festival
Carrying clocks the maidens come
Beautiful clocks tell perfect time
Happy Japan he sounds the water
Struck the bell and beat the drum
Flower forth order and civilization.

163   June 11   河童   Kappa

The boy ran over the bridge yelling
There in the water
We stared into the pond
A figure with long dank hair
Serpent eyes and a wide toothy grin.

164   June 12   Black Pepper

Wire mesh around poles
Filled with compost
Green columns
Clad with leaves
Tassles of abundant fruit.

165   June 13   Juneberry

Thy gentle finger shows me the fruit
A birthday present in June
A mass of white blossom in spring
In autumn the sunlight
Warmth in the reds such goodness.

166   June 14   소나무   Sonamu

Considering the russet browns
Soft red amber browns
Old fox-pelt browns
Auburn coppery browns
Seville-marmalade ginger tomcat browns.

167   June 15   叡山電車   Eizandensha

The trolley on the wire sings
The barrier at the crossing speaks
The wheels beat a rhythm on the line
Step by step we climb the hills
North out of Kyoto bearing west.

168   June 16   夏椿   Summer Tsubaki 1

The globe rounding
Swelling to bursting
Moist white petals
Smooth silk satin
The flower to open O what joy

76

169　June 17　Poplar

Under the pleasant trees
The oak, terebinth and poplar
In the cool breeze on the hill top
They set up a place of prayer
Look at this still standing.

170　June 18　夏椿　Summer Tsubaki 2

My flower gone in a day
Pity the brevity
I will put forth another
And another
Say I am yet undefeated.

171　June 19　三徳山　Mitoku Mountain

Through the red gate into the woods
Along the stream under the ferns
Great roots upon the slope
Climb pilgrim to the green height
The cloud between the giant cedars flows.

172   June 20   Myrtle
Take a myrtle wreath
Sing a line from the path
Passion no fruit desire to ash
The bays about thy head
Sing love the sky love the earth.

173   June 21   鳳凰   Fènghuáng
From out of the West you flew
Bird of Paradise
You rest with wings uplifted
You wait for me still
I shall see you on the water surface.

174   June 22   Crape Myrtle 1
Pursued by Ovid you became a tree
Shouting out aloud
Stop that   I like it
Your words flowered
Poet can it blossom any other way?

175   June 23   姫早百合   Himesayuri
Early to blossom princess
Rose in thy heart
Gentle mind
Long to continue
Love in word unselfish deed.

176   June 24   Tree by Water
Gracefully the slender branches touch the water
In between them goes the moorhen
The wind fills the sail
We tack across the broad
Wide skies of pale-blue and far away clouds.

177   June 25   仁淀川   Niyodogawa
Rain on the height
Wake me to life
Fill the blue pool
Speak from the cliff
A line of white thunder.

178   June 26   枇杷   Biwa
Loquacious fruit saying
May the truth be worshipped
Light-orange lamps are lit
My heart is filled with gladness
Joyful monkey finds you on the tree.

179   June 27   Begonias
Not supposed to have a favorite
Look at all these   so versatile
Olive leaves and tunic scarlet
Red-veined leaves and yellow
White blooms flushed with pink.

180   June 28   Pupa
Within these quiet walls
Every moment my thoughts changing
Dreaming of the green becoming
The sky wears a robe of stars
Between the sky and earth to fly.

181   June 29   Lily

Long white trumpet
What do I hear
The golden Tridentine
Russian & Greek sonorant
Coptic psalms in Arabic & Solomon.

182   June 30   Kuchiko

On the taut string the moist orange
Forms a dripping flag
The air will glaze them
Golden-red
There will be food for our family.

183   July 1   千鳥   Chidori 1

Keen a flowering love you sing
Thou art indeed a most strange
Long-limbed bird with blue eyes
A plover on the beach calling
Chiri chiri chiri   ya   chiri chiri!

184   July 2   Papillons

Chimney sweepers in black crepe
    Common blue in sky
Cabbage white unsteady flight
    Peacock catch my eye
Flowers my world in butterfly.

185   July 3   Ta'amia

Grind the chick peas to a pulp
Whiz and mash the fava
Mince the herbs in
Scoop the paste in little balls
Fry them up till brown and crisp.

186   July 4   Fynbos

There had been a burn the year before
It took away the fynbos
Flaming orange
A bed of ash and cinders
Look there now I see the Agapanthus.

82

187   July 5   鱧   Hamo
Awaji brought the eel to Yasaka
Lithe muscle-rope of strength
Out of the dark green sea
The life of the land
Pale white flesh in a festival bowl.

188   July 6   千鳥   Chidori 2
Let the barrel be a bird
Not a burden
A barrel of laughs
Heave it on my shoulder
A great round good sake barrel!

189   July 7   Mulberry
The weight of the ripe mulberry
It rests on my palm
A throne
Like a vintage wine
Love for you in our duty in time.

190   July 8   Hayabusa
Run a circle round the sun
Our paths intersect
What I give you
Secrets from a far
Carry home bright traveller.

191   July 9   Pearl
A perfect word spoken
The face is very bright
Light shows the clouds
Brighter than the stars
It is a wonder of wonders.

192   July 10   吉祥草   Kichijōsō 1
Still in the black earth
Roots pull deep
Will to flower rod of glory
Sceptre in hand
Orb arising my authority.

84

193   July 11   Great Purple 1

Through school stages I go
My horns in the music of wisdom
Turning brown I sleep in the leaves
Green again I grow and grow
From a beautiful house I will wing.

194   July 12   Karasu-uri 1

The sap capillaries
The bud bursts open
The lace filaments
Stretch suddenly out
White hand in moonlight.

195   July 13   Frogmore Gardens

In prayer walking the graceful lawn
Shadows of their spirits with me
Here my child admire the water
English clouds sail happily
Be peaceful child we made thee this.

196   July 14   Snowy Egret
Walking in the uplands
A soft undulation
The ground carrying water
Day of sun in monsoon
There she stood like a white bird.

197   July 15   Bougainvillea
A vine of purple bracts
Ran up the Jacaranda
Clouds in sunset
Magenta tents
Thunder bring me rain.

198   July 16   Jet
Flaps.   *Thrust.*   **Pitch the nose up**
Earth gone I'm in the wind
Short slender wings
Tilting turning
Clean lines.

199   July 17   Gion Festival
Tower high on great wheels
Maiden dancing on the shrine
Drum boom & pipe shrill
The men pull
Shouting   Washoi!   Washoi!

200   July 18   Trees
The oak in the field is a round hat
The western cedar a candle flame
The willow hides in a green veil
The Atlas cedar dances
The Scots pine lifts up her hand.

201   July 19   Phosphoresce
Little spirits
Climb the tree
Glowing green
Sing to me
Happily.

87

202   July 20   山百合   Yamayuri 1

Of my love for thee
I took the pistils
Wrote on the paper
Pressed the petal
The dew left this word.

203   July 21   山百合   Yamayuri 2

Not a wand but an armful
A cradle of perfume
Turn and say
Who are you
All these flowers for me?

204   July 22   山百合   Yamayuri 3

She will stand still most silent
Slowly turn her hand raise
Pure elegance
My senses take in perfume
Dance the lily upon the stage.

88

205   July 23   Kirin 1
Pardon me your Highness
Rushing to the left
You in a hurry
Your robes aflame
Are you fleeing or pursuing?

206   July 24   Kirin 2
Gobi Bactrian
Mohair married unicorn
Himalayan Yeti done a Yak
Are those scales reptilian
Did you say Giraffe?

207   July 25   Kirin 3
Though you don't belong
In a book of flowers
I raise my golden glass
Bright liquor foaming white
Auspicious Qílín flower in my book.

208   July 26   Mugunghwa 1
What names are given
Saint Joseph's rod
The Rose of Sharon
The Rose Mallow
Eternity flower in thee.

209   July 27   Mugunghwa 2
Methanol extract
Tested on wounds
The torn pages
Contracted and healed
The bright face is restored.

210   July 28   Mugunghwa 3
Round white sails
The petals fine paper
The red and white
Let the poem speak
A voice of friendship.

211   July 29   西瓜   Suika 1

Look at the fluff
Silver in light
New-born
Tender down
The first growth.

212   July 30   西瓜   Suika 2

Chiganemaru thy blade
A wave along the blue
Opens on the board
The perfect sphere
Let us share the gift with all.

213   July 31   西瓜   Suika 3

Bright thy face arise today
Sunfilled hours warm thee
Life within begin today
Great in hope arising
World thou art of joy to me!

214   Aug 1   栄螺   Sazae 1

Comes everything
Out of your house
Invisible miracle
Too big to see
Where's your beginning?

215   Aug 2   Kitano Tenmangu Festival

We found ourselves in the shrine
Called for sake and music
The girls danced and sang
The wine took me by the hand
My voice rang upon the walls in joy.

216   Aug 3   Oud

The prince bowed in greeting
His gilded waistcoat had jewels
His perfume took my senses
The rich balsam of Oud
Fragrant as the Prophet's word.

Peace flower with Islam! الله

217   Aug 4   Mountain Spring
Heart in the cold airs
Bright upon Hie
Flower in ice
Shaved in the lathe
Cumulonimbus on a plate.

218   Aug 5   Flag
Golden dove with soaring wings
She clasps the victory laurel
Palms beam forth in glory
I found a happy message
Hidden in the words.

219   Aug 6   飴細工   Amezaiku
Up the slope past the festival booths
Happy crowd of kids
A soft lump of sweetness
Deftly clipping to & fro
Joy it was a dragon then he did a corgi.

220   August 7   Globe & Streamers
They dance in the happy breeze
Festivals meet in blessing
The children of the children
Sweat pours from the men
Another year is blest in continuity.

221   August 8   Identifying
The other side of the room
Chocolate aroma
They were impressed
Harris tweed, alpaca, serge
I've always known what you wear.

222   August 9   Peace Flower
Gather them from here & there
Learn about Japan together
Along the way to know you better
Knowing you well I will know peace
In the pond a flower will bloom.

223   August 10   Time Square
They were dancing in the square
Hands above the head
Calling out
Stepping on like a wave
All in perfect time & all joined in.

224   August 11   Hoverflies
Striped like a wasp & wafer-thin
The light body of the hoverfly
Her unfeathered oars vibrating
Right-angled to the body held
Parallel to the lovely open flower.

225   August 12   Manga Flower
Through the portals of imagination
The world of desire
Graphics
Saying what I cannot say
The line riots & the colors flower art.

226   Aug 13   Cacao Pod 1
Held in my hand
Split
In two
Milky pap
Father says children.

227   Aug 14   Cacao Pod 2
A green and golden pod
Give birth and feed
He opened it
A wonder
Unknown to the ancients.

228   Aug 15   千年   Thousand Years
They gave the kids a project
Find a village older than a thousand
I started walking in my mind
Leaning on a Welsh stone wall
Gazing on a hill in Nara.

229　　Aug 16　　父ちゃん　　Totchan
Small wee voice shouting
Here I am you fool
On the can
Wearing a white tunic
Crest of three gold leaves.

230　　Aug 17　　大山　　Daisen
A carton of milk
I got it from high pastures
Thinking on early days
Digging up the ground
I found ancient bones.

231　　Aug 18　　Tobacco
Open the memory sachet
Was it Golden Virginia
Sweet fragrant leaf
Havana on my upper lip
I breathe in the richness.

232   Aug 19   Ainu Flower 1
Voices rise and fall around we go
Ancient spirit be sent forth
Let the Ainu flower
Old words our blood warm
Wa with us build our northern home.

233   Aug 20   Ainu Flower 2
The women hammer out the chant
The two girls lift up garment
Making wings flapping
Round they circle borne aloft
The old nations dance a family dance.

234   Aug 21   Ainu Flower 3
In winter the sea will freeze white
The cranes dance
In spring the bears awake
In autumn salmon climb the rivers
Wa with us defend the land we love.

235 Aug 22 真名井滝 Manai Waterfall

Alone I flew from the high bridge
It was a heaven-granted dream
Into the clear waters breathing
Climbing the down-pouring thunder
My body quivering & voice shouts in joy.

236 Aug 23 愛の輪 Ainowa

Youngsters with various challenges
We meet to learn about Japan
Bonding friendship cross-culture
Solving problems, growing stronger
Love for one another is the golden ring.

237 Aug 24 Matsuage Festival

Basket on the top of the pole
Ten men high
Hurl the flaming ball
Up in the sky
Night turn to Day in festival.

238   Aug 25   Cloudman
Potter with a lump of white
Round on round
Spinning
Building a shape
Great white castle in the sky.

239   Aug 26   Waxflower
These were the seals
The wax flowers won't melt
Not the hot sand   nor the dry wind
Not the sliding snake   nor the greedy man
Nothing can take away the land from our hope.

240   August 27   晒菜升麻   Sarashina Shōma
You stink in my nose
Herb you take away heat
Leaf gave me salad in spring
Now your fragrant fingers are waving
Calling the small souls to joy and peace.

241   Aug 28   鬼瓦   Onigawara 2
Don't you remember? We were 12
You opened the secret cabinet
Stole the vintage port
And we drank it behind the shed
That is exactly what he looked like.

242   Aug 29   Faith Flower
Allies in the struggle
Love one another and live
Let us tell the children
Choose a flower to love
Water your flower.

243   Aug 30   栄螺   Sazae 2
The round pail above me
I hunt the floor
All in one breath
Many thousand years
Bountiful ocean thank you.

244   Aug 31   Drums

Talk talk says the Noh drum
Sand in your hair mutters the snare
Doom da gloom bang a bass
Thunder done me wonder
Wadaiko leap in the sky.

245   Sept 1   杜鵑草   Unnamed

Utterly I refuse to tell them your name
Just let me say that when I saw the parcels
Like perfect parachute pods
I had no foreknowing
How strangely beautiful you'd be.

246   Sept 2   Crowberry

The heather drowses
The granite quartz sparkles
Bees hum and the hour dreams
Patiently one by one I am a Pict
Gathering berries in the sun.

247   Sept 3   台湾杜鵑草   Taiwan Hototogisu
Blush mauve
Prim lips purse
Unfurl six petals
The pistils fountain
Purple speckled white candle.

248   Sept 4   椎茸   Shiitake
Sit beside the log
Watch on time-lapse or
Hour by hour see the brown hat
Dance upward to a round roof
A brown hut   my harvest home.

249   Sept 5   Fishing Boats
Blue-green the sea-surface slides
Panels of steel melt in water
The black-hull fisher slow
Slow through the water
Pushes thru the sea glides over.

250   Sept 6   Hokkaido
Small knobbly earth-fruits
Short slivers fall from the peeler
Dark-brown Hokkaido earth
Cold in my hand marble white
Mashed with a lump of golden butter.

251   Sept 7   Brugsmansia
All was quiet in the large hall
As we stood there waiting
Without a sound
From the chandelier
A ghostly figure in a long white gown.

252   Sept 8   Phenom
The engines whistle up
The runway lights arrow
Leave the earth for the sky
In an hour it will be dawn
There on the rim the light appearing.

253 Sept 9 榎 Enoki 1

Planted on highways
How far to go now
Mysteriously named
Small orange cherries
The birds of the air rejoice.

254 Sept 10 Fig 1

Fig pollination
A total fabrication
How could it be true?
Tiny little wasps
Creeping out to put pollen in?

255 Sept 11 Night Fishing

The engine rumbles, bangs and groans
The wake widens behind us
The sun sets
The light-arms raised all round
Flickering silver fills the heavy seine.

256   Sept 12   Stormgods 1
The roof goes from east to west
Dark-grey herd of wild horses
Gallop from the ocean
Pulling behind them the billowing
Roaring stamping dancing gods of storm.

257   Sept 13   Stormgods 2
Oho aha the mighty drums
Great feet clap the floor
Ba Ba Ba the voice
Split the dark instantly
Light writing bright courses.

258   Sept 14   Stormgods 3
Oooh aaah the sac is opened
Hand of the sky
The pine trees hold the ground
Go through good wind
Bring the season bring the joy.

259   Sept 15   新幹線   Shinkansen
Smooth white alabaster thy aero body
Massive strength within you sleeps
Your arrival shakes the platform
You take me inside you
Bolt of blue we run through Japan.

260   Sept 16   Fig 2
    This little life
  I sat   quietly
A ripe fig   flushed purple
  A tiny   spider
    I crawled out.

261   Sept 17   Harvest
The fields were golden
Rice straw lifted to the sun
Tho I didn't want the harvest done
Preferring to reverse the time
Let them stand forever golden.

262   Sept 18   竹   Bamboo 1
Walk through the bamboo forest
Listen to the leaves rustle
Whisper and shuffle
The canes together rattle
Tattle talk tall tales to me of old.

263   Sept 19   竹   Bamboo 2
Forest of green bamboo
Knock on the hollow
The spirit sounds
A white flare
Columns stand in the yard.

264   Sept 20   竹   Bamboo 3
Seasoned in the weather
Coiled in the iron cauldron
Split each plat to a splint
The lines joined up with silk
Hang on the wall catch the sun.

108

265   Sept 21   White Dove

There's a princess with doves
One sitting on her head
She's laughing
Wearing orange trousers
A flock of doves flew after her.

266   Sept 22   Rushes

Strewn on the hard floor
The people kneel on the green
Harvest festival we thank the Lord
The house smells sweet
We bless the Lord for his great goodness!

267   Sept 23   Crab Apple

Jam jars on the white tiles
Red jelly in clear glass
A rose window
Mother made them
They were her best vintage.

268   Sept 24   Ebisu 1

Under your arm a golden bream
Fishing in Akashi Town
You stole the sign
Dancing upside-down
Cool golden liquor for my thirst.

269   Sept 25   Ebisu 2

Get Ebisu from the super
She said to me
When we were courting
I meet her again
Flowers to me the memory.

270   Sept 26   Islands

On the horizon
Sailing in time
Great carriers
Eastward Ho!
You first I follow.

110

271   Sept 27   興福寺三重塔   Kōfukuji
Built to hold his holy bones
A chamber of life
The walls crowded with flowers
The boys were laughing
Every word he spoke was wisdom.

272   Sept 28   ゆ   Yu
On the cool north side of the hills
A pool releases steam in the glade
Three figures robed in black
Splashing & singing
Yu wonderful yu.

273   Sept 29   藤袴   Fujibakama
In the small white pot
I probe my pipe
A drop of gold
To plump my wings
To brighten my day with joy.

274　　Sept 30　　生花　　Ikebana 1

Stare at the artwork
It comes to life
Spreading its arms
Regard to my right
Her flowering mind.

275　　Oct 1　　生花　　Ikebana 2

To tell you the perfection of the flower
I will let the flower sing
According to the laws of the flower
In the flower's own truth
Not the flower but the flower flowering.

276　　Oct 2　　生花　　Ikebana 3

By flower arrangement
There is meaning
Letters and characters
Heaven and earth
The flower is a teacher.

112

277   Oct 3   生花   Ikebana 4
I assembled a panoply of smell
I painted fragrance
On a board
Flowers and stinks
Lift it and sniff it odor Ikebana.

278   Oct 4   檜扇   Hiōgi
The leaves hide her secret smile
In sunlight her mottled glory
By afternoon her seed-pod swells
By evening she opens in beauty
The lacquer on her hair shines black.

279   Oct 5   鵯上戸   Hiyodori Jōgo
A tangle of autumn vines and leaf
Red and green globes side by side
My heart remembers the flower
A star arrived on earth trailing cloud
A sunrise in my heart this hopeful year.

280   Oct 6   郁子   Mube

Purple potatoes hanging in the air
What are you doing there?
Jungle delices
Swinging an orangutan
Man! These are good can I have some more?

281   Oct 7   円椎   Tsuburajii

I gathered you as treasure
Roasted in the bonfire
Here I find you
In mountain woods
Good bread you fed my people.

282   Oct 8   岩蓮華   Iwarenge

Modest in my hope
Lowly in my station
Stubborn in endurance
And when the time is right
I am a pillar of ambition to the sky.

114

283   Oct 9   Citron
Green capsule turn yellow
Remember the flower
Open the box
Seedtime and harvest
Thou fragrant white candle.

284   Oct 10   Abundance
The leaves are golden
The heads are silver
A long tassle
The field is full for harvest
We were blessed by the sun.

285   Oct 11   Wind
The fude lightly touches the paper
A fine unbroken line loops
And returns inviting
The wind 風
To stir through the field of cosmos.

286   Oct 12   Harvesters 1
Handles like a dream
Turns on a pin
Line by line
Shovels it in
Shakes it and packs it all trim.

287   Oct 13   Harvesters 2
The whole village
Cutting and stacking
Threshing and gathering
Laughing and groaning
How weary we were!

288   Oct 14   Harvesters 3
Specks in the eye
Stalks in the ear
Chaff in the nose
Bits in the collar
Filling the truck with gold.

116

289   Oct 15   Ginkgo 1

Eighteen thousand yellow flags
All the days I gave thee
Fly the flags in the autumn sun
I thank the Lord who sent me
My bones will rest beneath the tree.

290   Oct 16   Ginkgo 2

The leaf is printed on a stone tablet
Grand walker through the years
Tell me what you have seen
Grant me thy tenacity
Bright figure!

291   Oct 17   Ginkgo 3

Though the cliff crumble beneath me
Though the bells fall silent
Though the song stills
I put out roots into the air
I will sing forever the lauds of creation.

292   Oct 18   山黄櫨   Yamahaze
Coppery-bronze spear blades
Harvest the sap for lacquer
It burns like fire beware
The seeds give good oil
The candles burn bright.

293   Oct 19   Sumac
Dried and crushed
Ground to a spicy tang
When the powder leaked
The block of white marble
In the hold blushed deep.

294   Oct 20   Japan Flower 1
What am I to thee?
Mother of Japan
Flower of peace
The white cord
The words for love 愛 I learn.

118

295   Oct 21   Japan Flower 2
Shall we go back in time
Look what I found
A face for tomorrow
Eyes of a poet
Compassion for the world.

296   Oct 22   傘寿   Sanju
Stairs go up behind you
Descending or ascending
Light on each step
How well you have your hair
Your kimono a beautiful tone.

297   Oct 23   薄   Susuki
A black lacquered box
Silver chains tied round
The waves leap through the sea
The hillside bathed in moonlight
Light behind a rainfall as it falls.

298   Oct 24   荻   Ogi

The old man's hair and beard
Has he lost his large black hat?
Look at the white hair waving
How strong the wind and bracing
Whistling Nikola Nikola Nikolai-ii.

299   Oct 25   Fuji Ringo

Slender white fingers I admired
Fuji ringo you hold
Then you sang
Gentle song of autumn
The year to spring still you sang.

300   Oct 26   Akashiyaki

A golden globe
A promise inside
A piece of joy
Thank you
Old red baldy big round Dad with legs.

301   Oct 27   Autumn Maple
The first frost gripped my ankles hard
The leaf sugars go to anthocyanin
My hands stiffen out in crimson
Colder still the blood shrinks
All my leaves in protest shout to heaven.

302   Oct 28   Autumn Cherry
The leaves of the cherry turn autumn
The wind helps them fall
One by one
Glad be I now that they go
Gentle the wind and softly to rest there.

303   Oct 29   万作   Mansaku
A clown with a paper streamer
A dancing boy
Wave your hands and caper
Yellow and red
Roar with laughter we love you.

304   Oct 30   Tororo

Long pale brown hairy limb
How far you reach under land
To the family beginning
How hungry we were
Saving our lives.

305   Oct 31   踊り   Odori

Observe the precision of the fingers
Curving they write an arc
Pointing to the heart
A story they tell
Of discipline and patience in her art.

306   Nov 1   Mozuku

How the sweet chestnut
Resembled mozuku
Splitting open
You laughed
The brown inner gleams.

307   Nov 2   Kaede Momiji 1
They put scalding lights under the maples
The flames against the night sky
Looking for quiet
I walk with you again in memory
The leaf on the moss a pattern of my life.

308   Nov 3   Kaede Momiji 2
Sunset flung her robes upon the trees
Can I bear this glory
In the room the one I love
Patiently he sits waiting for me
Will you not love me as you promised me to?

309   Nov 4   Kaede Momiji 3
Calling on myself for inspiration
The small grey stone figure
A red leaf before him
Where's the poem
Cut the shape out into light.

310   Nov 5   Kaede Momiji 4
How cold it is this morning
There's frost in my blood
One final effort
One huge breath and give
Give scarlet vermillion give red.

311   Nov 6   樮   Buna
The wind polished the sky
Waiting for dawn
The sun rises
Pouring the light in the beeches
In the pond the unburning flames.

312   Nov 7   小菊   Kogiku
A field of yellow flowers
Chrysanthemums
菊の花 kiku no hana
The Niigata plain
Sent me a dish of sunshine.

124

313   Nov 8   吉祥草   Kichijōsō 2
Planted in the garden to bring joy
Small mauve and white flowers
Unnamed in English they say
Small red fruits like garnets
Call it "Joy-in-our-children."

314   Nov 9   Takeda Castle
It is cold at dawn in the eyrie
The cloud fills the long valley
Thermos of hot tea and biscuits
The sun will burn away the mist
Look there a hawk is flying south.

315   Nov 10   Satsumaimo
Bright minerals Kirishima
Warm weight in my palm
Endure the gestation
Bubbling boiling vaporing
Vitality pure glass of life.

316   Nov 11   Coffee 2
A wicker basket of ripe coffee beans
Glossy red coral beads
The milky heart
Roasted to chocolate
Small cup black gold sweet to heaven.

317   Nov 12   言葉   Palavras
Jingle joyfully I ring the bell
Quietly beside me
Little voices chiming louder
Ringing with laughter
Words in funny-accent Portuguese.

318   Nov 13   Karasu-uri 2
Galaxies without number
Light years hang a veil
The years come round
They pull the veil away
The green fruit is now red.

319   Nov 14   Japanese Maple
The names make a poem
Japanese 楓・紅葉
Latin is a truth
English another truth
In China it is called *the chicken-claw*.

320   Nov 15   Akashi Nori
Pulling on the red net roller
Fixing the net with spores
Twenty meters waving in the sea
The green-black nori
Lengthens its dark-green hair.

321   Nov 16   Kosode Koshimaki 2
Ask me the meaning
Worlds I am wearing
Lives I have lived
Petals unfolding
The changing-unchanging.

322 Nov 17   Single Malt
Pale gold amber
A cold fog on Islay
Sea-salted & enflamed
Tars and oak resins
Thou heart-warming friend!

323 Nov 18   Nori Seaweed
Haul the nets from the Inland sea
Purple triangles in the sky
Little black beards
Vat the black   stir it round
Press it in sheets & stamp it true 明石.

324 Nov 19   Sushi
My eyes follow the rapid folding
The rice embraced into form
The bream sliced in a single curve
The dance continues in rhythm
The sushi lined up in perfection.

325　Nov 20　菊の花　Kiku no Hana
A jar of water
The window sunlit
Light in the liquid
Still clear still bright
Chrysanthemum.

326　Nov 21　秋明菊　Shūmeigiku
Spotlight from the cloud a hold
There you are
In the eyes of the regarding
Mie in your new name
Old self new self the true you.

327　Nov 22　Taylor
With one look you apprise him
Hunting the perfect seam
Diving into waves and appearing
500 fabrics on my shelves
The suit you wear is a work of art.

328   Nov 23   榎   Enoki 2
The tree grew peacefully in the forest
The gentle moss in the quiet air
For nearly a thousand years
Green leaves and fruit
Who could not say you are holy.

329   Nov 24   和紙   Washi
Pasha! Pasha!
The pale water sloshes
The glue thickens and shines
Thirty times he tilts & tips it
Behold the finest in Japan.

330   Nov 25   Akashi Tako Senbei
Old red baldy boiled soft
Chopped in bits
Rice powder paste
Pressed and fried
Tako Crackers shout for joy!

130

331 Nov 26 舞踏 Butoh

Learn wisdom
The miracle of life
Out of darkness
Twisting in the spotlight
We are born and reborn.

332 Nov 27 Ballet Flower

Will no one dance it properly
Must the movement be stiff
The fan uplifted without joy
Must she shake her legs
As though they're covered in ants?

333 Nov 28 沖ノ島 Okinoshima 2

Early days in a good wind
Friendships unrecorded
We lifted cups in joy
We told no one
Gifts we gave look here.

334   Nov 29   Crab
蟹 life you are giving
Fearsome armored friend
Guardian with mighty clippers
Sideways we go dancing
Wave an arm   rattle a leg.

335   Nov 30   町家   Machiya
Old road in the Kobe hills
A derelict inn at the crossroads
Locals raise a fortune
Restore the fabric, tidy the garden
Kanpai! To the ghosts of Edo Japan.

336   Dec 1   Aurora 1
The air was dry & completely clear
Snow crunched as we stamped
A palpitation through the sky
Gossamer danced and flickered
The light in aurora was a rainbow.

337   Dec 2   Winter Jasmine 2

On the trellis dark green shoots
Buds appear as red fruit
Bursting in bright yellow
Brightens the winter wall
In winter sunlight summer sun.

338   Dec 3   Rice Bowl

   steam   息
 from   出
 rice   飯
 pray   謝
   thanks 日

339   Dec 4   First Ones

Tribal conflict drove us eastwards
Walking with all we possess
Moving out of reach
Look the red-face is laughing
Bones melt in the good brown earth.

340   Dec 5   福玉   Fukudama
Hemispheres of rice
Sakura and plum
New Year within
Happy you marry
Joyful birth you become.

341   Dec 6   海老蔵   Ebizō
The family business is art
Painting signs in the air
Generations take the name
Thinking of you mother father
Japan I fly in the light with my son.

342   Dec 7   Encourager
Boldly she spoke
Small acts
Kindness shown
Whoever & whatever
The time has come to speak.

134

343 Dec 8 養命酒 Yōmeishu 1
A tonic to restore me, to raise the life in me
Cinnamon warms my fingers
Cloves clear my hurt, safflower brightens
The mother wort speeds the pulse like a stream
Turmeric inspirits my natural strength.

344 Dec 9 養命酒 Yōmeishu 2
Second dose of tonic with epimedium
Blood rushes to my nose
My nostrils dilate
The hair in my eyebrows
Itches & I look about with youthful urges.

345 Dec 10 養命酒 Yōmeishu 3
Du Zhong to calm me
Don't run around like a dog
Another sip to strengthen me
Don't bark at her, don't bite
Down boy! Climb a tree & sing.

346   Dec 11   Puzzle 2

Struck the head against the black
Broke the yolk in a bright spurt
The word sputtered into flame
The wood shrivelled
The dark could not contain me.

Peace flower with Islam! الله

347   Dec 12   芝翫   Shikan

High voice sings in the nose
All eyes upon her
Onnagata
How you move me
Flower before us your high art.

348   Dec 13   Aurora 2

In the arctic sky
A red conflagration
Glowing and pulsing
The refracted sunlight
Billowed like a curtain.

349   Dec 14   Puzzle 3

Shall I follow a star on lovely wings
Or sit patient
Or spring forth in strength
Or with you
Wise Rajah   lift me up to the world.

350   Dec 15   Hot Sake

As the warmth moved through me
The snow on the great thatch
Shifted, I remembered
The blue-tiled roofs
The brown cypress roofs of Kyoto.

351   Dec 16   湯たんぽ   Yutanpo

I find an old friend
There's no rust on you
She filled you from the kettle
You waited for me
I slide within how warm.

352   Dec 17   備前   Bizen

How the light runs along the blade
The old excitement I felt
Powerless at the gate
Wild dogs are they
With thee I could stand against them.

353   Dec 18   広辞苑   Kōjien

Looking for a friend
To share a glass with
I open the good book
I find a letter from you
Happy hours in your garden.

354   Dec 19   Teacher

Help me to understand
Count the rings on my finger
You point to the sky
Look with X ray eyes
I see what you are.

355   Dec 20   Brahms Flower
Time beside us calls the dance to end
Round we go lifted on the wind
In your eyes I find my hope
My happiness you send
Time away be gone there'll be no end!

356   Dec 21   Hot Water Bottle
Old rubber belly
Hard to fill
She showed me
Boiling from the kettle
Turn the plug the cold sheets warm.

357   Dec 22   Solstice
Druids cut the mistle from the oak
On the darkest day of the year
The fruits promise light
In New Grange he lays a shaft
Deep in the dark he wakes the stone.

358   Dec 23   Happy Birthday
Majestic dragon on a gold coin
Talon holds the soul of good
Talon reaches on the right
Talon reaches out to left
Talon reaches far back to the tail.

359   Dec 24   Gratitude
The charities came to lunch in the Mall
Mother Teresa of Calcutta made a saint
We cannot all do great things but we can do small
Head bowed   thank you to the Queen
Bow more deeply   thank you to her friend.

360   Dec 25   猿   Saru 1
Red-faced
Arms hanging on the edge
Phew it's hot **you say** *Whew*
Family got their arm around
I can love you Saru.

361   Dec 26   猿   Saru 2

It is Christmas time
I am in the forest when it was cold
What can we give you
What have we done brave friend
Thou who lived all these ages in Japan?

362   Dec 27   猿   Saru 3

The forests have all but gone
Each in his own world
Hunting his selfish need
If we cared or loved
We'd work together & solve.

363   Dec 28   Celebration

Great swollen bladders
Huge round bellies
Worlds with fuse
Blasted upward
Exploding stars & rainbows.

364   Dec 29   Peace Maker
A time for honeyed odes to lift up praise
A god to grant me eloquence to speak
For thy victory today a golden olive
Songs like the cosmos I adorn you
A garland of flowers for the king.

365   Dec 30   Skytree Tokyo
Arm in arm
Round we go
In a tall Tower
A miracle tree
Happy with you.

366   Dec 31   花火   Hanabi
The children cried out with high voices
From out of nowhere it came
Rings of rainbow color
Orange I saw and sapphire blue
A moment it stays there above us it blooms.

367   Epilogue Poem: 華   Hana

Look up there
Read the flowering line
In the fluid running
The flowers open
The tender vine sings thy praise.

Run then with thy nose through the fields
Label the smells and scents each one
Flowers beauty in God's benison
The cornucopia of smell
Fill thy joy.

The pads of your fingers
Touch the petal
Gently now
The nerve-endings
Glow and sing to the brain.

Poem Number and Note

1. A reply.
2. A reply.
3. 源氏物語・雲隠六帖「夢の世に幻の身の生まれ来てうつつ顔にて過ぐし果てめや」.
4. 火花 hibana, spark in Japanese, lit. fire-flower.
5. Anthesis (Grk) "flowering" or "full bloom."
6. Inspired by New Year Karuta (poetry cards) in Yasaka Jinja, Kyoto (Jan 2017).
7. This ancient custom continues today. Originally from China.
8. Oenanthe javanica. Capsella bursa-pastoris. Lapsana apogonoides.
9. Explaining "Hotokenoza 仏座."
10. Turnip. Daikon. Stellaria media. Gnaphalium affine.
11. Dawn time. A verse inspired by the kanji character 櫻 sakura cherry.
12. Prewar poster of Asahi Beer, a maiden lifting up a beer bottle.
13. 足立美術館庭園. Adachi Bijutsukan Garden, Shimane.
14. Ancient Shrine 宗像大社 Munakata Taisha, Okinoshima, Fukuoka.
15. Amygdalus communis. Shaqed (Hebrew) root meaning "awake, alert."
16. A camellia, or a rose.
17. Jade was a talismanic life-giving stone from ancient times.
18. Tea-seed oil, brown rice, and green tea make Genmaicha.
19. Also called capsicum or sweet pepper.
20. Inspired by cockerel in Isonokami Jingu 石上神宮 Tenri, Japan.
21. Pan-fried Chicken. White Sinapis alba or S. arvensis. Black Brassica nigra.
22. 淡路市岩屋・絵島 Awaji Eshima・ref. 西行 Saigyō 「千鳥なく絵島」.
23. 天道様 Tentō, principal god, sun. 丹波篠山黒豆 Tanba Sasayama Kuromame.
24. Wakame harvested 和歌山県由良町白崎 Yurachō, Wakayama.
25. Japanese wild boar, sliced and presented as a peony (or a rose).
26. Remembering my first years in Japan. The local tofu-maker. Hankyu Express train.
27. See Stean Anthony, *One Hundred Poems*, poem 4; *Manyōshū 365*, poems Jan 8, Feb 24 & Dec 2.
28. 葉ニンニク Garlic leaves used to make nuta sauce. Susaki Kōchi 高知県須崎市.
29. Party leader Renhō 蓮舫 attends Diet wearing modern kimono 20170120.
30. Inspired by the Crown Prince Hironomiya (Naruhito) New Year poem 20170114.
31. Inspired by the Crown Prince Hironomiya (Naruhito) New Year poem 20170114.
32. 平成 Heisei name announced in Jan 1989.
33. Imagine a priest who stands for all the family. "Fuku wa uchi." Happiness in home.
34. Matsuo Taisha Iwamikagura 石見神楽 Setsubun performance Feb 3.
35. Susanoo (deity) defeats 8 headed snake. Finding of sword Kusanagi no Tsurugi.

36. The maiden says thank you to Susanoo (deity).
37. 平成 Heisei name had a wide appeal.
38. Japanese era name 年号 nengō or 元号 gengō, given for each Imperial reign.
39. Inspired by Manyōshū poetry. In the original a young girl gathers herbs.
40. Seeking inspiration from ancient poetry.
41. Jasminum nudiflorum. 黄梅 ōbai.
42. 六甲山・七曲滝 Rokkō Mountain Nanamagari waterfall freezes.
43. 1000 years. 奈良長谷寺 Nara Hasedera Dadaoshi Fire Festival Feb 14.
44. Coffea arabica. Coffee originated in Ethiopia.
45. Buddhist saint 源信 Genshin (942-1017) teacher & founder. Sixth Patriarch.
46. Remembering my first years in Japan. Kyoto plum blossom covered with snow.
47. Nara Hasedera Dadaoshi Fire Festival Feb 14.
48. 岡山西大寺裸祭り Nakedness Festival men compete to be "happy man" 福男.
49. 水戸市・偕楽園・梅花・Plum blossom festival Feb-March Mito City. Prunus Plum.
50. Bonsai competition red and white plum blossom first prize.
51. Daphne odora. 沈丁花 Jinchōge. Princess Fawzia Fuad of Egypt (1921-2013).
52. Poem for Japan-Brazil. Emigration 1908 from Kobe. Omamori is a talisman.
53. Puzzle poem. What is the Japanese word hinted at? Answer is: shinshi しんし.
54. Inspired by Empress Michiko using 「真摯 shinshi」『美智子様100の言葉』p. 180.
55. Inspired by onigawara outside Nenbutsu Temple, Arima 念仏寺有馬.
56. "For a Mother in England" (poet's mother). Reprinted from SM365.1.11.
57. Tulip. Consider early history of the tulip in Europe. See also SM365.3.47.
58. Tulip. Turkish lale, from Persian lale. In Arabic, lale has the same letters as Allah.
59. Plecoglossus altivelis. Swift-flowing unspoilt rivers were once common in NE Asia.
60. Brother Theo letter to Vincent Van Gogh, birth of son (31 Jan 1890). Vincent's imagined reply.
61. 白樺 Shirakaba Betula platyphylla var. japonica. Inspired by Tolkien.
62. 白樺 Shirakaba Betula platyphylla var. japonica. Inspired by Tolkien.
63. Craft doll made for Doll's Festival Hinamatsuri by Matsui Kōgeisha まつい工芸社.
64. Chinese indigo & safflower used for dyeing cloth.
65. Pyramid of Hinamatsuri dolls in 鴻巣市 Kōnosu City, Saitama. Feb-March.
66. 烏來瀑布 Famous waterfall and cherry blossom, Wulai, Taiwan.
67. Anemone coronaria. Mediterranean flower. A verse in an ancient style.
68. Anemone nemorosa. European wildflower.
69. Anemone pavonina. Mediterranean flower.
70. *Slam Dunk* (1990-1996) manga & animation by 井上雄彦 Inoue Takehiko.
71. 烏來瀑布 Famous waterfall and cherry blossom, Wulai, Taiwan.
72. Chinese coins found in archaeological dig, Minami Awaji. Dated c. 200 CE?
73. 神戸六甲山牧場 Kobe Municipal Rokkōsan Pasture, above Kobe City.

147

74. Omizutori ritual begun 752, 東大寺奈良 Tōdaiji, Nara.
75. First years in Japan. Purple Hankyu Train high-quality engineering.
76. Spectacular spring flowers in Namaqualand South Africa (October).
77. Inspired by potter 八木一夫 Yagi Kazuo (1918-79)「ザムザ氏の散歩」(1954).
78. Arab & Jewish schoolchildren for peace, Jerusalem 2002-12.   Kobe Peace Research Institute.
79. Making Japanese rice wine 酒 sake.
80. Origami Folding Together Peace Project.   http://kobe-peace.org/
81. 花大根 Hana Daikon. Hesperis matronalis. Mustard family.
82. Ancient sheath fold rock formations 南淡路島沼鞘状褶曲.
83. Buddhist monk sculptor of genius (??-1224) Nara & Kyoto.
84. Tōfu-making in Japan. 1000 years of history?
85. Thank you to MW online dictionary.
86. Properly called Christmas Rose or Black Hellebore. Helleborus niger.
87. Heike Monogatari "Atsumori no Saigo" Sumaura, Kobe.
88. Responding to a TV program about the suffering of children.
89. Osaka Naniwa Church (1930) founded by 澤山保羅 (1852-1887). Meiji saints.
90. Lignite formed from ancient forests, also called brown coal.
91. Remembering the sunset I saw when I arrived in Japan, 1986.
92. An ancient meaning of the name 富士 Fuji is "undying" or "eternal."
93. Linking the mainland to Awaji Island. "Pearl Bridge" in English. 1998.04.05.
94. Yamataka jindai sakura. Edohiganzakura variety. Hokutoshi, Yamanashi.
95. Nichiren Buddhist saint sits beneath an ancient cherry.
96. Unique beauty of the ancient shrine wooden construction.
97. Kyoto Gion Miyako Odori dance performance in April. Kyoto Maiko Dancers.
98. 華やか hanayaka: gorgeous, brilliant, splendid, gay.
99. 日本国際仏教興隆協会の印度山日本寺。 Bridge for peace between India and Japan.
100. 国宝・阿弥陀聖衆来迎図・平安時代・和歌山・有志八幡講蔵。
101. Enkianthus perulatus also called 満天星躑躅.
102. Visiting Tsubaki Jinja. Tutelary deity 猿田彦大神 Sarutahiko no Ōkami.
103. What is the word to hold? Puzzle poem for the word seishin せいしん.
104. Primula veris. Long tubular flowers with yellow petals.
105. Inspired by Alison Uttley, "Recipes from an Old Farmhouse" (1966).
106. Caltha palustris, called cowslip in the USA. Kingcup.
107. Imagine a contest with different kinds of shrub and tree. A blind friend speaks.
108. Vietnamese court music performance Tam Luan Cuu Chuyen. Unesco world heritage.
109. Capsicum annuum.
110. Garlic on my fingers after cooking.
111. Upheld. Prayer for peace.

112. Inspired by a detail of the decoration of Kasuga Taisha Nara (Aug 2016).
113. Inspired by a nesting icon egg & 重要文化財十一面観音立像.
114. Myrto Dimitriou teaching Origami on Greek TV.
115. Inspired by Geiko Natsuna & Maiko Momo dancing in Kyoto 夏菜・桃.
116. 坂東玉三郎 Bandō Tamasaburō V dancing the 羽衣 Hagoromo.
117. Nguyen Dinh Chieu Blind School performance attended by Japanese Emperor, Hanoi 20170301.
118. Planting a rose tree to celebrate Queen Elizabeth II 90th birthday 2016.
119. 神戸市立神港橘高校「競技龍舞」龍獅團 20170502. Shinkō Tachibana High School.
120. 藤原定家 Fujiwara Teika (1162-1241) & family. My grandfather's house.
121. Aralia elata. 楤の木 Tara no ki. Mountain greens eaten in Japan & Korea.
122. Bletilla striata 'Murasaki Shikibu.' Inspired by info. from botanyboy.org website.
123. Adapted from EM verse (2015)「君は光の中にいましき」. Original for Emperor Akihito. p. 148.
124. Chloranthus serratus. Shizuka Gozen. Nō dance, Bunraku & Kabuki. *Senbon Zakura*.
125. Spiraea cantoniensis. Festival 競馬会 Kurabeumae, Kamigamo Shrine, Kyoto (May 5).
126. Emperor Akihito and Empress Michiko visit kindergarten 20010507.
127. Convallaria majalis. Lily of the valley.
128. Used as a medicine. English garden in Surrey.
129. Inspired by rice-planting machines, Japan.
130. 碓氷第三橋梁 Usui Bridge, brick-built viaduct. Engineering achievements.
131. 小袖腰巻・浅井長政夫人・お市の方(1547-1583)像・高野山持明院.
132. Imagining peacock butterfly Aglais io. RSPB Otmoor (photo by Charles J. Sharp).
133. Homage to Ichikawa Ennosuke III & IV Kabuki theatrical splendor.
134. From seedling mat to rice-harvest, Japanese mechanical revolution.
135. Bubalus bubalis. Kyoto Matsuri. See also SM365.6.208.
136. Inspired by ancient mirrors 鑁・金粒珠玉象嵌宝相華紋鏡・六稜鏡・唐 8 世紀.
137. Homage to Tagore (1861-1941). Compare SM365.6.137. Inspired by Mary Austin (1868-1934).
138. Habenaria radiata. 鷺草 Sagisō. RSPB began with egrets. See SM365.1.213 & 356 & 2.125.
139. The subtle art of 吉田玉男 Yoshida Tamao I (1919-2006) Bunraku puppeteer.
140. 豊岡市辰鼓楼 clock tower Toyooka city (1871). 鶴 stork. Successful recovery.
141. Acorus calamus. Highly regarded plant from ancient times in China & Japan.
142. 万華鏡 & 萬花筒. Kalos beautiful. Eidos form. Kaleidoscope.
143. 葛飾北齋 Katsushika Hokusai (1760-1849) print. British Museum Exhibition 2017.
144. Black grouse. Indebted to Iolo Williams, *Nature's Home* (RSPB) (Autumn 2016) 98.
145. Inspired by 銀閣寺 Ginkakuji standing in a pine glade on an isle in the Inland Sea.
146. 大山 Daisen 鳥取県 Tottori. Anemone nikoensis. See SM365.3.104.
147. 国宝・法性寺 (924 CE) 千手観音立像. Senju Kannon, Kyoto (c. 934 CE).
148. Syringa vulgaris. Pronounce lilac in French.
149. What is the word hinted at? Puzzle poem for the Japanese word Omoiyari 恕.

149

150. Vincent Van Gogh's *Irises* 1889. Japanese Iris.
151. With the beloved in a Welsh wood, a walk in the hills.
152. Liriodendron tulipifera. Lily like flowers. Eastern USA. Trees grow up to 50 m.
153. Pioneer species making an environment for the oaks.
154. Syringa vulgaris. Lilac in the old English garden. With thanks to MSH.
155. Capsicum annuum. Cayenne pepper.
156. Farfugium japonicum. Remove 灰汁 aku (the bitterness) & enjoy.
157. Campsis grandiflora. "Morning Calm."
158. 唐招提寺・鑑真 (688-763) Tōshōdaiji Temple, Nara. Ganjin founding saint.
159. Hydrangea in the old English garden. Native flower of Japan.
160. 足立美術館庭園. Adachi Bijutsukan Garden, Shimane.
161. Piper nigrum. Vine. Black pepper harvested in Malabar, Kerala.
162. Time Festival, Ōmi Jingu, Otsu (June 10) 近江神宮大津市.
163. Kappa living in the pond of Tsujikawayama Park, Kurosaki, Hyogo.
164. Piper nigrum. Increasing pepper production in Kerala, India.
165. Amelanchier canadensis.
166. Pinus densiflora beautiful bark. 赤松 Japanese & Korean red pine.
167. Kyoto local train to Hieizan and Kifune.
168. Stewartia pseudocamellia.
169. From ancient times, humanity sought the divine in high places.
170. Stewartia pseudocamellia. 有馬念仏寺庭園. Nenbutsuji garden.
171. Buddhist temple 三佛寺 Sanbutsuji National treasure, Tottori mountains.
172. Myrtus communis.
173. 平等院鳳凰堂屋上の鳳凰像. Phoenix on roof of Byōdōin Temple (1053) Uji, Kyoto.
174. Lagerstroemia indica. 猿滑 Sarusuberi, name means "monkey slips."
175. Lilium rubellum. Rose lily. 姫 hime, princess.
176. Memory of sailing on the Norfolk broads.
177. Niyodo river in Shikoku.
178. Eriobotrya japonica. Loquat. English name from Cantonese 蘆橘 Lou-gwat.
179. This verse reprinted from Saint Mary 365.4.182. There are other flower poems.
180. This verse reprinted from Saint Mary 365.4.183. There are other flower poems.
181. Lilium longiflorum. Native of the Ryukyu Islands, Japan.
182. ナマコ・くちこ dried eggs of sea cucumber, local delicacy. 石川県七尾市.
183. Donald Keene performed as Tarōkaja in the Kyōgen *Chidori* (1956).
184. Odezia atrata. Inspired by Judy D. who talked about *Cymbeline*.
185. Falafel recipe. Popular food in Egypt, Israel, Syria.
186. Agapanthus praecox. African lily. Cape Peninsular. See SM365.6.155.
187. Muraenesox cinereus. Conger eel. Brought to Gion Matsuri from Awaji Island.

188. For Donald Keene his life-work a bridge for understanding Japan.
189. Inspired by verses by the Crown Prince & Princess Michiko (1959).
190. Inspired by EM verse. 「その帰路に己を」 Japanese spacecraft (2010).
191. Full moon appearing directly above Fuji, called "Pearl Fuji." July 2017.
192. Reineckea carnea. Said to augur good fortune to the house where it blooms.
193. Sasakia charonda 大紫 Ōmurasaki Great Purple Emperor Butterfly.
194. 烏瓜 Karasu-uri. Trichosanthes cucumeroides.
195. Gardens planted & tended by British Queens (Queen Elizabeth the Queen Mother et al.)
196. Habenaria dentata. See Botanyboy.org website. See SM365.1.213. Cp poem 138.
197. Bougainvillea glabra. Johannesburg SA.
198. 鴨か雁か。 In praise of the HondaJet (2016).
199. Old screen showing Gion Matsuri, Kyoto, early Edo period (c 1650).
200. Inspired by the shapes of the trees.
201. Mycena lux-coeli. 椎の灯火茸. 神戸市六甲山森林植物園.
202. Lilium auratum. Golden-rayed Lily, native to Japan.
203. Lilium auratum. Golden-rayed Lily, native to Japan. Also published in SM365.7.80.
204. Traditional dance. Inspired by 井上八千代 Inoue Yachiyo IV & V. 人間国宝.
205. Kirin Beer logo. Chinese mythological creature. 麒麟 Qílín.
206. 麒麟 Qílín is a creature of good augury. It is said to be a giraffe.
207. Kirin Beer logo red & white & gold. Kanji used: male 麒 female 麟.
208. Hibiscus syriacus. Korean name Mugunghwa 無窮花 Mugung, eternity.
209. 木槿 Mukuge. Mugunghwa (Korean). Said to have medicinal properties.
210. Hibiscus syriacus. Korean national flower. 韓国と日本の間に平和と愛咲くように。
211. Citrullus lanatus. Water Melon. The fruit develops.
212. Citrullus lanatus. Water Melon. 治金丸 famous royal Okinawan sword.
213. Citrullus lanatus. Water Melon.
214. Turbo cornutus.
215. A noble visits Kyoto, Edo period. 北野天満宮・東山遊楽図屏風.
216. Aquilaria agallocha, Agarwood, Oud (Arabic).
217. かき氷 Kakigōri made from water from a Hie Mountain spring, summer dessert.
218. Victory flag for 100th High School Baseball Championship, Japan (2018).
219. Festival candy sculptor. See Asakusa Ameshin & Amezaiku Yoshihara, Tokyo.
220. 短冊と球 festival bunting. Sendai Tanabata Matsuri Aug 6-8.
221. Someone wore cloth dyed brown with cacao. Identifying it, a blind friend speaks.
222. 平和の架け橋 Peace Bridge Project Israel-Palestine-Japan dialogue & friendship 2005~.
223. Inspired by 阿波踊り Awa Dance group 寶船 Takarabune dancing in NYC.
224. This is an old poem rewritten (Aug 1985). For hoverfly see SM365.2.206 & SM365.5.164.
225. Manga School Yokohama, Japan & Lucca, Italy - artistic traditions meet & thrive.

226. Cacao grown in ancient times in Soconusco, South Mexico.
227. By new discovery the New World prompted the beginning of modern science.
228. 耳成・畝傍・天香久・ Gwynedd, Ceredigion.
229. Supermarket shelf. Beer. 恵比須 Ebisu Japanese god of fishermen & good luck.
230. Inspired by the mountain Daisen, Japan & Yayoi archaeology.
231. Habanos cigars. Gauloises. Gitanes.
232. The Ainu of Japan are a North Pacific First Nation, Hokkaido.
233. North Pacific First Nations. Indigenous peoples. Alaska & Russia & Canada.
234. Success-story Ito Crane Sanctuary, Kushiro Shitsugen, old Ainu territory, Hokkaido.
235. 九州高千穂峡 Takachiho Gorge, Kyushu, Japan. Natural Monument.
236. Osaka charity Duskin Ainowa supporting international exchange for disabled persons, 35 years.
237. 愛宕神社 Hanase Kyoto. Festival for a good harvest & protection from fire.
238. Cumulonimbus capillatus.
239. Geraldton Waxflower. Chamelaucium uncinatum. Western Australian shrub.
240. Cimicifuga simplex. Actaea simplex. Bugbane genus. Butterflies and nectar.
241. Ogre tile decorating the Miiedō, Chion Temple, Kyoto 京都知恩院御影堂.
242. Need to protect principal places of worship with active monthly support.
243. 海士・海女 Ama diving for sazae with floating cedar tub on surface, 7m depth.
244. 和太鼓 Wadaiko traditional Japanese drumming performance art.
245. Tricyrtis hirta. Japanese Toadlily. See poem 247.
246. Empetrum nigrum. Northern harvest for native peoples and wildlife.
247. Tricyrtis formosana. See poem 245. Tricyrtis genus found in Japan & Taiwan.
248. Lentinula edodes. Speeded up film.
249. Calm waters, a scene on the Japan Sea.
250. 北海道産男爵. Praise for the Hokkaido Danshaku potato.
251. 木立朝鮮朝顔. Brugsmansia suaveolens. Angel's Trumpet.
252. Embraer Phenom 300 flying to the Caribbean.
253. Celtis sinensis. Japanese hackberry, also Chinese hackberry.
254. Ficus carica. Miracles in the natural world.
255. Inspired by YouTube clip about night fishing.
256. Typhoon season in Japan August to September.
257. Rainy season (monsoon) in Japan is June-July.
258. In western Japan storms can be quite powerful.
259. The Japanese Bullet Train, high speed rail (from 1964).
260. Inspired by 『水清魚見』有馬頼底 Arima Raitei *Torino* vol. 38 Spring 2016.
261. Looking on the fields of golden rice at the time of harvest.
262. Phyllostachys bambusoides. In praise of bamboo.
263. Inspired by a memory shared by 田中旭祥 Tanaka Kyokushō, bamboo artist (東京).

264. Inspired by bamboo-blind by artist artisan Cho Dae Yong (Korea).
265. Inspired by 2 photos of Princess Norinomiya (now Kuroda Sayako) with doves.
266. Old Churches had earthen floors, sweet-smelling rushes. Acorus calamus.
267. Memories of home.
268. God of fortune Ebisu. Sapporo Yebisu Beer. Upside-down Bream Akashi Station.
269. Memory associated with Sapporo Yebisu Beer.
270. Island nations & continents. Friendship & a line for peace.
271. Kōfukuji Pagoda Heian Nara first level flower-pattern vivid colors (1143).
272. Legend about 3 crows healed by hot spring, Arima, Kobe. 湯 ゆ yu, hot spring.
273. Parantica sita. Asagimadara. Chestnut Tiger. Butterfly on Eupatorium japonicum.
274. Inspired by Ikebana artist 池坊專好 Ikenobō Senkō (Ikenobo) with artwork.
275. Inspired by Ikebana artist 池坊專好 Ikenobō Senkō (Ikenobo).
276. Inspired by Ikebana artist 池坊專好 Ikenobō Senkō (Ikenobo).
277. Developing an Ikebana for the blind making art through smells.
278. Belamcanda chinensis. Blackberry lily. Leopard flower. ぬばたま.
279. Solanum lyratum. Japanese wild flower related to the tomato.
280. Stauntonia hexaphylla. Dessert fruit offered to the Imperial court in ancient times.
281. Castanopsis cuspidata. Chinquapin. Donguri. Acorns used as ancient food.
282. Orostachys iwarenge.
283. Citrus medica. Fruit (Heb. Etrog) used in the Jewish feast Sukkot. Sept-Oct.
284. Harvest fields of wheat & rice in the sun.
285. 書道 Calligraphy. Art turning verse into art. Cosmos bipinnatus.
286. 自脱型コンバイン Jidatsugata. Japanese rice combine-harvesters.
287. Inspiration from Iseki presentation on tractors and harvesters YouTube.
288. How it used to be before the combine harvester. Wheat & rice.
289. Saint Nikolai remembers the days he gave to Japan (1861-1912).
290. Ginkgo biloba, unique arboreal survivor, ancient fossils exist of the leaves.
291. Celebrating the ancient Ginkgo of Tiānmùshān 天目山.
292. Rhus sylvestris. Toxicodendron. Native tree Japan & China. Lacquer. Candle wax.
293. Rhus coriaria. Summaq means red (Syrian). Used to dye leather.
294. The poet looks at a photo (1958) of Empress Michiko.
295. *Time* magazine cover: 正田美智子 Michiko Shōda. March 23, 1959.
296. Empress Michiko palace photograph 80th birthday Sanju (2014.10.20).
297. Susuki. Japanese pampas grass. Miscanthus sinensis.
298. Miscanthus sacchariflorus. Amur Silver Grass. In honor of St Nikolai of Japan (Feb 16).
299. Homage to Shimazaki Tōson "First Love" 島崎藤村 「初恋」.
300. Akashi, Japan 1st prize gourmet food Octopus omelette (Dec 2016) 明石玉子焼き.
301. Acer genus, ranging from Momiji to Sugar Maple.

302. To everything there is a season. Eccl. 3.1.
303. Hamamelis japonica. Homage to 野村万作 Nomura Mansaku, Kyogen.
304. 自然薯 Jinenjo. Dioscorea japonica, native Japanese yam. Grated paste.
305. Inspired by Geiko Koai and Maiko Mamekiku dancing in Kyoto. まめ菊・小愛.
306. Nemacystus decipiens. モズク mozuku, brown filamented seaweed. Health food.
307. Acer palmatum. Irohamomiji. Visiting 東福寺 Tōfukuji temple, Kyoto.
308. Acer palmatum. Irohamomiji. Visiting 三千院 Sanzenin, Kyoto.
309. Acer palmatum. Irohamomiji.
310. Acer palmatum. Irohamomiji.
311. Fagus crenata. Japanese beech. 青森県十和田市蔦沼 Tsutanuma after typhoon.
312. Small edible Chrysanthemums.
313. Reineckea carnea.
314. 竹田城跡. Imagining a visit to Takeda Castle in autumn.
315. Kirishima satsumaimo used to make Shōchū liquor. 霧島焼酎.
316. Coffea Arabica. Coffee originated in Ethiopia.
317. Poem for Japan-Brazil. Emigration began 1908 from Kobe. Visiting a shrine.
318. 烏瓜 Karasu-uri. Trichosanthes cucumeroides.
319. Acer palmatum. 雞爪槭 jīzhuǎqī lit. The Chicken-claw Maple.
320. 明石のり. Nori seaweed is farmed in the 瀬戸内海, Inland Sea, Akashi, Japan.
321. 小袖腰巻・浅井長政夫人・お市の方 (1547-1583)像・高野山持明院.
322. In praise of the single malts, the true Scotch, without ice.
323. Harvesting nori seaweed from the Inland sea, 明石市 Akashi, Japan.
324. The artistry of sushi.
325. In honor of Prince Takahito of Mikasa (1915-2016). Grandson of Meiji.
326. Inspired by picture of flower in Buddhist nun Setouchi Jakuchō's garden. 襲名.
327. Inspired by 柴田音吉洋服店 Shibata Otokichi Kobe. Taylor from 1883.
328. Celtis sinensis. Natural Monument. 徳島県つるぎ町・国天然記念物.
329. 津山箔合紙 Tsuyama Hakuaishi. Washi made in Tsuyama, Okayama.
330. Octopus rice cracker (takosen) from Akashi. 明石蛸煎餅・永楽堂.
331. Inspired by the choreography of 天児牛大 Amagatsu Ushio (1949-).
332. Kitri variation Act 3, Don Quixote (solo dance).
333. Ancient North Kyushu & South Korea. Centuries of contact and trade, Fukuoka.
334. A message from the kanji 蟹 kani, crab.
335. Local initiative restoring old Japanese houses Machiya 町家. 淡河宿 Ōgoshuku.
336. Aurora borealis.
337. Jasminum nudiflorum. 黄梅 ōbai.
338. Cooked rice (御飯 gohan) steaming in a rice bowl (茶碗 chawan).
339. When did people arrive in Japan? Who were they?

340. Inspired by 藤谷攻 Fujitani Osamu, 進々堂 Shinshindō, Kyoto, making fukudama.
341. Ichikawa Ebizō XI (39) with son (4) flies on wire, Kabukiza, Tokyo July 2017.
342. Inspired by Queen Elizabeth II Christmas Message 2016.
343. Japanese tonic with spices. Popular in Japan. Dating from 1602.
344. Cinnamon, Clove, safflower, turmeric, Siberian motherwort.
345. Epimedii herba (Epimedium) & Eucommiae cortex (Du Zhong).
346. An old poem I rewrote (from c. 1981).
347. 中村芝翫 Nakamura Shikan VII, Kabuki artist (1928-2011) & family.
348. Inspired by a photo of the aurora above the Showa Arctic research station.
349. See Kanematsu matchbox design, swallow, peach & elephant. 兼松日産農林マッチ.
350. Kyoto, Miyama, kayabuki thatch. Hiwadabuki cypress bark roof.
351. Old Japanese hot water bottle, shaped like a bottle.
352. Bizen sword 「山鳥毛」 (c 1300) (Uesugi Kenshin's sword).
353. In praise of 新村出 Shinmura Izuru (1876-1967) dictionary editor.
354. 東寺・五重塔・Highest wooden building in Japan 55 m. Tōji, Kyoto (826 CE).
355. Johannes Brahms (1833-1897). Hungarian Dance 5.
356. Remembering mother filling the hot water bottle.
357. Ancient faiths, Celts of the British Isles and New Grange, Ireland.
358. Inspired by a gold coin issued for the Emperor's 83rd Birthday 20161223.
359. QEII Xmas Message 2016. Hana Book 1 says thank you to Queen Elizabeth II & His Majesty Emperor Akihito.
360. 猿 Saru Japanese native monkey in the mountain hot spring.
361. 猿 Saru Japanese native monkey. Let us remember the defenceless ones.
362. 猿 Saru Japanese native monkey. A message for today.
363. Firework balls made by Ichiyama Co. 市山煙火商会・徳島小松島.
364. Inspired by Pindar's "Olympian Ode 11."
365. Inspired by Emp. Akihito and Empress Michiko visiting Tokyo Skytree 20120426.
366. Inspired by the work of Dr. Amano Akiko 天野安喜子 Hanabi (firework) artist.

Profile

Stean Anthony

I'm British, based in Japan. I've written a series of books of poetry promoting understanding and peace. Find out more from the list at the end of this book. I have also published *Eco-Friendly Japan*, Eihosha, Tokyo (2008). *Monday Songs 1-7*, and *Eitanka 1* (pdf file textbook freely available on website – and sound files). Thanks to Yamaguchi HT & MK for kind help.

New Projects

Enarchae (story in short paragraphs)
Hagios Paulos 4 (songs on the theme of Saint Paul)
Hana 2 (verses on theme of flowers & other things)
Heiankyō 2 (translations of classic Japanese poetry)
Saint Mark 339 (translation of Gospel into Japanese verses)
Saint Mary 365 book 7 (verses dedicated to the BVM)
Sport 2 (verses on the theme of sport)

Author's profits from this publication to be donated to the maintenance and improvement of small city parks in Japan and UK.

Stean Anthony Books with Yamaguchi Shoten. Original poetry & translations & adaptations. Most are textbooks.

- *Selections from Shakespeare 1-5* (selected passages)
- *Great China 1-4* (translations of classical Chinese poetry)
- *Kŏngzĭ 136* (poems based on the sayings of Confucius)
- *Manyōshū 365* (translations of ancient Japanese poems)
- *One Hundred Poems* (inspired by 百人一首 *Hyakunin Isshu*)
- *Heiankyō 1* (translations of ancient Japanese poems)
- *Inorijuzu* (Buddhist & Christian words for peace)
- *Sufisongs* (poems for peace in Jerusalem)
- *Soulsongs* (poems for peace in Jerusalem)
- *Pashsongs* (songs & poems by Stean Anthony)
- *Bird* (poems on the theme of birds)
- *Sport* (poems on the theme of sport)
- *Songs 365* (poems based on the Psalms)
- *Songs 365* (translation into Japanese pdf available)
- *Songs for Islam* (poems based on verses in the Koran)
- *Isaiah Isaiah Bright Voice* (poems inspired by Bk of Isaiah)
- *Saint Paul 200* (poetic phrases from the *Letters of Paul*)
- *Hagios Paulos 1-3* (poetry based on life & letters of St Paul)
- *Gospel 365* (based on the Synoptic Gospels)
- *Saint John 550* (poetic version of the Gospel of St John)
- *Saint John 391* (translation to Japanese of *Saint John 550* Gospel)
- *Saint John 190* (transl. to Japanese of *Saint John 550* Catholic Letters)

- *Saint Matthew 331* (translated into Japanese verse)
- *Saint Luke 132* (chapters 1-2 in Japanese verse)
- *Saint Mary 100* (poems dedicated to St Mary)
- *Saint Mary 365 Books 1-6* (calendar of poems on themes relating to Mary, Holy Mother, flowers, icons, prayer, scripture)

- *Messages to My Mother 1-7* (essays on faith and other things)
- *Mozzicone 1-2* (essays about questions of faith & other things)
- *Monday Songs 1-7* (pdf textbooks of English songs)
- *Eitanka 1* (pdf textbook teaching poetry)
- *Psalms in English* (75 lectures in English teaching the Psalms pdf textbook). Pdf are freely available.

- *Exnihil* (story written in short paragraphs)

HANA 1
by Stean Anthony

Company : Yamaguchi Shoten
Address : 4-2 Kamihate-cho, Kitashirakawa
Sakyo-ku, Kyoto, 606-8252
Japan
Tel. 075-781-6121
Fax. 075-705-2003

HANA 1 定価 本体2,000円（税別）

2018年5月20日 初 版

著 者　Stean　Anthony
発行者　山 口 惠 子
印刷所　大村印刷株式会社
発行所　株式会社　山口書店
〒606-8252京都市左京区北白川上終町4-2
TEL:075-781-6121　FAX:075-705-2003
出張所電話　福岡092-713-8575

ISBN 978-4-8411-0941-2　C1182
©2018 Stean Anthony